THE MATE RELATIONSHIP

SUNY series,
Human Communication Processes

Donald P. Cushman and Ted J. Smith III, editors

/ THE MATE RELATIONSHIP /

Cross-Cultural Applications of a Rules Theory

Anne Maydan Nicotera

STATE UNIVERSITY OF NEW YORK PRESS

Production by Ruth Fisher
Marketing by Bernadette LaManna

Published by
State University of New York Press, Albany

For information, address the State University of New York
Press, State University Plaza, Albany, NY 12246

Library of Congress Cataloging-in-Publication Data

Nicotera, Anne Maydan, 1963-
    The mate relationship : cross-cultural applications of rules
theory / Anne Maydan Nicotera.
        p.   cm. — (SUNY series, human communication process)
    Includes bibliographical references and index.
    ISBN 0-7914-3543-1 (hc : alk. paper). — ISBN 0-7914-3544-X (pb :
alk. paper)
        1. Interpersonal communication—Cross-cultural studies.
    2. Interpersonal relations—Cross-cultural studies. 3. Mate
selection—Cross-cultural studies.   I. Title.   II. Series.
    BF637.C45N463   1997
    153.6—dc21   97-500
                                                                      CIP

10   9   8   7   6   5   4   3   2   1

For my son

Edward Nicotera Maydan

Teddy, whom I birthed with this book,
who continually gives me rebirth

CONTENTS

PREFACE

This book is an application to several American and two non-American cultures of a general theory that we recently tested and extended (Nicotera and Associates, 1993). In this previous book, *Interpersonal Communication in Friend and Male Relationships*, we derived seven testable propositions from Cushman and his associates' general theory of interpersonal relationship initiation and development: (1) Perceived self-concept support is the basis of interpersonal attraction; (2) Different types of perceived self-concept support are the bases for different types of interpersonal relationships; (3) Different types of self-concept support are the bases for *entry* into and increasing *intensity* of interpersonal relationships; (4) The type and form of self-concept support is homogeneous by culture; (5) Conflict that threatens self-concept support on crucial relationship variables—the lack of it or attacks on it—is the most potentially dangerous type of conflict in interpersonal relationships; (6) Negotiation of differences in perceptions of self-concept support on crucial relationship variables cements interpersonal relationships; and (7) Quality interpersonal relationships consist of intimacy, personal growth, and effective communication on the crucial relationship variables.

In Nicotera and Associates (1993) we directly tested and supported the first four propositions. The work in this second book applies those four propositions to several cultures and explores two others (5 and 7—it was considered premature to launch a study of 6 until 5 had been fully investigated). In the process, attributes and levels of mate relationships are identified and tested for several cultures. The research contained in this second volume increases the depth of the work by examining several American co-cultures, one Caribbean culture, and one Asian culture, and extends the breadth of the work by moving beyond the first four propositions. Thus, this volume has both theoretical and cross-cultural value. The chapters are somewhat redundant, as they contain parallel studies, but as they are separate studies each needs to be able to stand alone.

The first chapter reviews the general theory, presents research questions, and describes the methodology for all the studies. Chapters Two through Six present studies that apply the first four propositions to different cultures. The seventh and eighth chapters explore Propositions 5 and 7 in English-using cultures. The final chapter offers interpretations, conclusions, and speculations—grounded in an emphasis on the multi-cultural view afforded by the general theoretic structure. Implications for intercultural mate relationships are addressed, and directions for future research are suggested.

The work behind this project has been long and sometimes tedious. Several people were invaluable in bringing it to fruition. Foremost, I thank all those involved in the administration of Howard University's Faculty Research Support Grant (FRSG) program. This project was funded by FRSG for two years and would have been a much longer process without such support. I especially thank Mr. Leonard Clay, FRSG budget director, for his tireless patience. I thank those of my colleagues in the department of Human Communication Studies at Howard University who are always willing to give that little extra. Two graduate assistants were invaluable in doing library legwork: Dr. Amardo Rodriguez, now on the faculty at Purdue University, and Ms. Paula McKenzie. My gratitude is also extended to those who assisted with data collection: Dr. Lyndrey Niles, Dr. David Woods, Dr. Jennifer Keane-Dawes, Mr. Timothy Thompson, Dr. Jamey Piland, Ms. Joylene Griffiths-Irving, and Mr. Chris Cowlin. Finally, thanks to Ms. Allyson Wattley for the final proofreading.

No book about mate relationships should be produced without acknowledging the often overlooked but crucial role of the author's own mate. Gregory Maydan, my best friend and so much more, has throughout the years unfailingly provided me with self-concept support on crucial attributes—exactly as described by the theory. In fact, part of what has driven my work in this area is the extent to which the theory continues to ring true with my own fortunate experience of being a partner in a high quality mate relationship.

In closing this preface, it is important to re-emphasize that the chapters represent applications of the theory described in the first chapter and developed in the previous work (Nicotera and Associates 1993). There is still much to be done in this line of work and in analyzing how this research tradition fits in with and contributes to the broader personal relationships literature. This volume is merely the beginning of the theory's application cross-culturally.

Anne Maydan Nicotera

CHAPTER ONE

GENERAL THEORY, PROPOSITIONS, AND RESEARCH QUESTIONS REGARDING MATE RELATIONSHIPS

Purpose

This chapter begins with an overview of the theoretic propositions driving this research effort, presents specific research
questions derived from those propositions, and describes methodologies for the studies that are presented in subsequent chapters.
In a recent body of work (Nicotera and Associates 1993), Cushman's
rules theory of interpersonal relationship development (Cushman
and Cahn 1985; Cushman, Valentinsen, Dietrich 1982) was tested
and extended. Seven testable propositions were derived from the theory (see Table 1.1), four of which were directly tested and supported.

In the process, attributes and levels of friend and mate relationships were identified and tested for several cultures. The extensions accomplished by Nicotera and Associates (1993) consist of
those propositions that expand the theory into the areas of relational conflict, maintenance, and deterioration. The research contained in this second volume, focusing exclusively on heterosexual
mate relationships, increases the depth of the work by examining
several American co-cultures, one Caribbean culture, and one
Asian culture, and extends the breadth of the work by moving
beyond the first four propositions into the areas of conflict and
relational maintenance. In so doing, several research questions
(RQs) were developed; these are presented below. Before present-
ing these RQs and describing the methods by which they are
explored, however, basic overviews of the rules paradigm and of

1

Table 1.1 Propositions derived in Nicotera & Associates, 1993

Proposition 1. *Perceived self-concept support is the basis of interpersonal attraction.*

Proposition 2. *Different types of perceived self-concept support are the bases for different types of interpersonal relationships.*

Proposition 3. *Different types of self-concept support are the bases for entry into and increasing intensity of interpersonal relationships.*

Proposition 4. *The type and form of self-concept support is homogeneous by culture.*

Proposition 5. *Conflict which threatens self-concept support on crucial relationship variables—the lack of it or attacks on it—is potentially the most dangerous type of conflict in interpersonal relationships.*

Proposition 6. *Negotiation of differences in perceptions of self-concept support on crucial relationship variables cements interpersonal relationships.*

Proposition 7. *Quality interpersonal relationships consist of intimacy, personal growth, and effective communication on the crucial relationship variables.*

the general theory are presented. These two overviews draw heavily from the first chapter of Nicotera and Associates (1993).

Paradigmatic Assumptions

For our purposes in discussing interpersonal relationships, the most central of paradigmatic assumptions is the shift from a positivistic view of humans as reactors to a view of humans as actors. The rules perspective, as an alternative for communication theorists, was introduced by Cushman and Whiting (1972). Rooted in symbolic interactionism and speech act theory, the rules perspective was intended to move the field of communication away from its preoccupation with laws and positivism. The rules perspective conceives of human beings as conscious, teleological actors who choose to enact specific behaviors based on their goals and the structure of the social rules that govern and guide the specific situation (Cushman and Pearce 1977; Cushman and Whiting 1972).

The primary assumption in the rules perspective is the action principle: Social behavior is structured and organized. Action within and between human beings is not random. Humans govern their actions by implicit and explicit rules. Finally, choice is involved in social action. According to Cushman and Pearce (1977), rules take the form of the practical syllogism:

A intends to bring about C;
A considers that to bring about C s/he must do B;
therefore, A sets her/himself to do B.

The possible range of actions (B) is delimited by the social rule structure. The practical syllogism illustrates the perspective's epistemological assumption of a normative order in the regularities of human action (Cushman and Pearce 1977).

Human behavior is classified into two categories: Movement and Action (Cushman, Valentinsen, and Dietrich 1982). *Movement* can be defined as habit and is governed by nomic necessity, which accounts for reactive behavior and depends on a causal relationship. *Action* is evaluative, purposive, and choice-oriented and is governed by practical necessity, which accounts for proactive or teleological behavior. Action is further classified into *information processing*—perception or thought—and *coordination*—consensus among individuals (Cushman *et al.* 1982).

In coordination situations, the basic unit of analysis is the standardized usage (Cushman *et al.* 1982). Acting in concert, individuals coordinate a standardized usage for social rules. The rule structure is either created through negotiation or recognized as a previously existing rule structure (Cushman and Whiting 1972). Regardless of its origin, the standardized usage is of primary interest to the rules theorist, since it defines the set of alternative choices for behavior (B in the practical syllogism above).

Characteristics of a standardized usage are as follows: First, a shared class of intentions; second, a common set of expectations; and third, sequences of communicative acts that demonstrate the level of commitment to the standardized usage (Cushman *et al.*, 1982). According to Cushman and his associates (Cushman and Cahn 1985; Cushman and Craig 1976; Cushman and Florence 1974; Cushman and Pearce 1977; Cushman *et al.*, 1982), all human actions necessarily involve rules. Furthermore, all actions requiring coordination with others involve communication and, therefore, communication rules. Rules theorists identify two types of rules:

Constitutive rules, which specify the action's content; and *procedural* rules, which specify appropriate strategies for carrying out the action (Cushman and Whiting 1972).

Given this conception of human action, *interpersonal relationships can be seen as coordination systems* (Cushman *et al.* 1982). The function of these systems is to develop and maintain consensus on individual self-concepts. Their structures are dyadic relationships, specifically friend and mate relationships. Their processes center around the development, presentation, and validation of individual self-concepts (Cushman *et al.* 1982). Below is a discussion of Cushman's general theory of the role of communication in interpersonal relationships, which is grounded in the rules perspective and focuses on self-concept and interaction as the generative mechanisms of relationship formation and growth.

General Theory of the Role of Communication in Relationships

Filters

In their seminal work on relational development, Kerckhoff and Davis (1962) posit that relationship development progresses through a series of filters, usually conceptualized as stages. Several of the first theories of mate relationship development were based upon this notion (e.g., Knapp 1978; Lewis 1972, 1973; Murstein 1972, 1977; Nofz 1984). Cushman and his associates (Cushman and Cahn 1985; Cushman *et al.* 1982) formulated a more complex theory of relationship development, beginning with a three-step filtering process for relationship development. First, individuals are faced with a *field of availables*. This field consists of all the others with whom it is possible to form a relationship. In this same time period, research that explored initial interaction (typified by Berger and Calabrese 1975; and Duck 1976) showed such interaction to be governed by standardized and general communication rules (Cushman *et al.* 1982).

Within the field of availables, there exists the second filter, the *field of approachables* (Cushman and Cahn 1985). This field consists of all the others whom the individual finds desirable enough to approach for the purpose of initiating a relationship. A particular set of *entry rules*, explicated below, guide such relationship initiation. Within the field of approachables there exists the third filter, the *field of reciprocals* (Cushman and Cahn 1985). This field consists of those who have reciprocated the individual's attempt to initiate a relationship. These are the people with whom the individual has interpersonal relationships. A particular set of *intimacy/intensity rules*, explicated below, guide the growth of these relationships. Once relationship pairs have been filtered to the field of reciprocals, they progress through several relationship levels. Traditionally, casual date, steady date, fiancee, and spouse have been the level designations studied. However, in the current work, the labels for relational stages are considered an empirical question because Nicotera (in Nicotera and Associates 1993) was unable to find adequate support for the four traditional labels.

The Role of Self-Concept Support

The original theory (Cushman and Cahn 1985; Cushman and Craig 1976; Cushman and Florence 1974; Cushman *et al.* 1982) identified self-concept as a cybernetic control system for human action in coordination situations:

> Human actions that take place within a standardized communication situation require common intentions, an established set of rules for the cooperative achievement of those intentions, and a procedure for manifesting the variable practical force the actors feel for participating in the coordination task. (Cushman et al. 1982, 96–97)

Self-concept is an empirically verifiable construct that provides a theoretical representation of the conceptual forms through which individual actors understand and cope with the world. The construct *self-concept* thus allows the exploration of the link between thought and action (Cushman *et al.* 1982).

The nature of self-concept. Self-concept is composed of self-object relationships, which are divided into three classes (Cushman *et al.* 1982). First, the *identity self* includes self-object relationships that label what an individual *is*, such as "I am a teacher." Second, the *evaluative self* includes self-object relationships that declare one's feelings about oneself, such as "I am a good teacher." Finally, the *behavioral self* includes self-object relationships that prescribe appropriate behavior for the identity- and evaluative selves, such as "I am a good teacher and therefore I must have my papers graded on time" (Cushman *et al.* 1982, 98).

Self-concept thus aids the individual in coordination situations in three ways (Cushman *et al.* 1982). First, the individual's encounter with an object provides information that can be generalized to other objects s/he categorizes in the same *class*. Therefore, s/he need not have an encounter with an object in order to define the self in relation to it. Second, such self-object relationships provide the individual with *expectations* for the nature of those objects s/he subsumes under the same rules. Finally, the self-concept, as it develops, provides the individual with *preconceived plans* of action (Cushman *et al.* 1982).

> A self-object relationship constitutes a ready-made format for processing experience and initiating action. With such a system, a person is prepared to cope with the future and make sense out of the past. Hence, we regard the self-concept as an organized set of structures that defines the relationship of objects to individuals and that is capable of governing and directing human action. Furthermore, the self-concept, as an organized set of structures, provides the rationale for choice in the form of a valenced repertory (sic) of alternative plans of action. (Cushman et al. 1982, 98)

Self-concept and interaction. A primary coordination task for any individual in a communication situation is the development of intentions (Cushman and Florence 1974). These are represented by *C* in the practical syllogism. Likewise, the individual must develop the means for achieving those intentions (Cushman & Florence, 1974). These action alternatives are represented by *B* in the practical syllogism. These intentions and the acts that achieve them are integral to the most basic coordination task—determining the self, who the individual is and how s/he relates to objects (and others) in his/her environment (Cushman and Florence 1974).

The development, presentation, and validation of self-concepts is generally accepted as a central feature of the process of interpersonal communication (following Cushman and Cahn 1985; Cushman and Craig 1976; Cushman and Florence 1974; Cushman *et al.* 1982). The function of interpersonal communication systems is to regulate consensus with regard to individuals' self-concepts; the structure is provided by "the standardized code and network rules that guide how and when we can obtain consensus in regard to preferred self-object relationships" (Cushman *et al.* 1982, 104). In interaction, individuals propose identities for themselves and others. These identities are negotiated in interaction: an individual learns who s/he is and what s/he can do in the presence of certain others. *Thus the self-concept, as it is developed, presented, and validated in interaction, defines the nature and type of the interpersonal relationship.*

This logic led to the postulation that "reciprocated self-concept support serves as a necessary basis for establishing any interpersonal relationship" (Cushman *et al.* 1982, 104). It follows that different types of self-concept support lead to different kinds of relationships (e.g., friend or mate), *and* that different degrees of self-concept support lead to different levels of interpersonal relationships (e.g., casual date or steady date). (Cushman *et al.* 1982) provide a thorough and cogent review of research literature grounding their conceptualization of self-concept.)

The role of self with mates.   A mate has been traditionally defined as an opposite sex other for whom one clears the field of competitors (Cushman and Cahn 1985; Karp, Jackson, and Lester 1971). (Work is ongoing which applies the theory to same-sex mate relationships.) For the development of an opposite sex mate relationship, the theory posits five *entry rules*, applied to the field of approachables (Cushman and Cahn 1985, 57–58; Cushman *et al.* 1982, 109–110).

1. The greater an individual's perceptions that an opposite-sex other is physically attractive, the greater the likelihood of initiating communication aimed at establishing a mate relationship.

2. The greater an individual's perceptions that an opposite-sex other's real-self relates to one's ideal-self for a mate, the greater the likelihood of initiating communication

aimed at establishing a mate relationship.

3. The greater an individual's perception that the male's real-ideal self-concept discrepancy is small, the greater the likelihood of initiating communication aimed at establishing a mate relationship.

4. The greater an individual's perception that an opposite-sex other is likely to accept one's offer of a relationship, the greater the likelihood of initiating communication aimed at establishing a mate relationship.

5. The more frequently an individual provides messages that (a) manifest self-concept support for an opposite-sex other's physical attractiveness; (b) characterize that other as relating to the individual's ideal-mate; and (c) indicate a perceived lack of discrepancy between the male's real and ideal self, the greater the likelihood that the other will perceive those messages as an attempt to initiate a mate relationship.

For the field of reciprocals, the theory posits two *intimacy/ intensity rules* (Cushman and Cahn 1985, 58; Cushman *et al.* 1982, 111).

1. The greater the female's perceived lack of discrepancy between her mate's real and ideal self-concept, the greater the likelihood the relationship will grow.

2. The greater the perception that there is reciprocation of self-concept support, the greater the likelihood the relationship will grow.

The seven propositions in Table 1.1 were developed because the rules posited by the general theory are not explicitly confirmable or deniable. The propositions are derived from the conceptual theory and the literature on mate relationships (reviewed in Nicotera and Associates 1993). *All these propositions can be directly traced in conceptual origin to the theoretic work presented in Cushman and Cahn (1985, especially pp. 5–100). As such, these propositions are **not** to be considered original theory; rather, **they represent specific empirical statements of the general conceptual theory as originally developed by Cushman and his associates** (Cushman and Cahn 1985; Cushman et al. 1982).* The propositions are easily operationalized and supported by the literature and by the studies in Nicotera and Associates (1993) and in this volume.

Research Questions

Proposition 1, that perceived self-concept support is the basis of interpersonal attraction, is treated as an assumption, given the strong direct support found in the previous research (Nicotera and Associates; see also Bailey and Helm 1974; Bailey and Kelly 1984; Bailey, Finney, and Bailey 1974; Bailey, Finney, and Helm 1975; Buss and Barnes 1986; Cahn 1986; Crawford 1977; Helm, Bailey, and Vance 1977). For all the cultures studied, two research questions were posed to discover the *culturally-specific* attributes and levels of mate relationships, upon which to base subsequent RQs.

RQ1a: What are the attributes of mate relationships (in each culture examined)?

RQ1b: What are the levels of mate relationships (in each culture examined)?

Proposition 2, that different types of perceived self-concept support are the bases for different types of interpersonal relationships, is not addressed in this research. Given the strong and direct support offered by the previous research (Nicotera and Associates 1993) for this proposition, it was considered more fruitful to extend the depth of the work by focusing on one type of interpersonal relationship—the mate relationship.

Proposition 3, that different types of self-concept support are the bases for *entry* into and increasing *intensity* of interpersonal relationships, is also treated as an assumption because of the support offered by the previous work (Cushman and Cahn 1985; Cushman *et al.* 1982; Nicotera and Associates 1993). For all the cultures studied, the following research question was posed to discover the *culture-specific* nature of the attributes elicited by the pursuit of RQ1a, above.

RQ2: Which attributes are entry and which are intensity variables (in each culture examined)?

Proposition 4, that the type and form of self-concept support is homogeneous by culture, is also treated as an assumption (Nicotera and Associates 1993). This assumption can be confirmed by noting the commonality within and the diversity between the cultures studied regarding the first RQ.

Proposition 5, conflict that threatens self-concept support on crucial relationship variables—the lack of it or attacks on it—is the most potentially dangerous type of conflict in interpersonal relationships (based on Genshaft 1980; Levinger 1980; Rands, Levinger, and Mellinger 1981; Ritter 1985; Ting-Toomey 1983), represents one of the extensions of the work offered by this volume. The validity of this proposition is explored with two research questions. Given the exploratory nature of this research and problems with translation, these RQs are applied only to the cultures studied in English-speaking countries (i.e., American co-cultures and Jamaica, but not Japan).

RQ3a: Is the absence of self-concept support on crucial relationship variables related to relational disintegration?

RQ3b: What are potential sources of conflict for each level of mate relationships and for mate relationships in general?

Proposition 6, that negotiation of differences in perceptions of self-concept support on crucial relationship variables cements interpersonal relationships (based on Billingham and Sack 1987; Birchler, Weiss, and Vincent 1975; Cushman 1989; Cushman and Cahn 1985; Genshaft, 1980; Gottman, Markman, and Notarius 1977; Noller 1981; Rands et al. 1981; Ting-Toomey 1983), is not tested. The converse of this proposition implies that when partners' differing perceptions of self-concept support cannot be successfully negotiated, the relationship will be weakened and eventually destroyed. This reasoning follows from Proposition 5, and the process could be studied under the realm of relational maintenance and/or repair. To adequately examine this process, we would need to obtain detailed accounts of relational conflict from several cultures. Given the labor-intensive nature of such research, it was considered imprudent to embark on such research prior to a complete test of Proposition 5. Until we are more sure about the attributes of relationships as sources of conflict, focusing on the management of such conflict is premature.

Proposition 7, that quality interpersonal relationships consist of intimacy, personal growth, and effective communication on the crucial relationship variables (based on Aguirre and Kirwan 1986; Cushman 1979; Cushman 1989; Cushman and Cahn 1985; Fincham and Bradbury 1989; Montgomery 1981; Rettig and Bubolz 1983; Spanier and Lewis 1980), is explored with the following RQs. As with Proposition 5, these RQs are applied only to the cultures studied in English-speaking countries.

RQ4: Is relational quality related to intimacy, personal growth, and effective communication on the crucial relationship variables?

RQ5: Are there other factors that can be identified as important for relationship quality in different cultures?

Method

Sampling

Each study used two samples; specific descriptions of the samples are provided in the appropriate chapters. Five cultural groups were sampled from a variety of colleges and universities. Three are American co-cultures: White Americans of European descent; African Americans; and Deaf White Americans of European descent. The other two cultural groups were from Jamaica and Japan. The population most commonly studied in this line of research has been college students.

Though we cannot generalize beyond this population, we must not assume that such sampling diminishes the work...(While in college many individuals meet) their future spouses. Regrettably, the population of that same age that does not attend college remains untapped...However, for study of relationship development, college student samples are highly appropriate. At that time in our lives we are most active in developing friendships and mate relationships. The college experience, like almost no other, provides constant opportunity to meet and spend time with a great number of one's peers. From the close proximity of living quarters and the semester-to-semester shift of classmates to the overwhelming number of organized social activities, the college campus offers a seemingly boundless field of availables. This is a perfect setting in which to study relationship development. (Nicotera and Associates 1993, 224-225)

White Americans represent the lion's share of the population of "Americans" who have been surveyed in this research tradition. Because the researchers conducting the work have until now been faculty at predominantly white institutions, the American college student samples of convenience have been mostly white. In fact, research in this tradition has, until now, failed to differentiate American co-cultures, treating all Americans as a single culture. This may be one of the reasons Nicotera (in Nicotera and Associates 1993) was unable to find intracultural homogeneity for mateship levels in her American sample.

In fact, there is no discernable "American culture." The United States, as a multicultural society, is made up of several-coexisting cultural groups. This fact leads to the use of the term "co-culture," which connotes the coexistence of several cultures in American society, rather than the term "sub-culture," which connotes that there is a larger, superordinate culture that predominates and is privileged over lesser "sub"-cultures.

All three American samples were drawn from universities in the Middle Atlantic region of the United States. The White American samples were drawn from a large state university; the African American samples from a middle-sized Historically Black University (HBU); and the White Deaf samples from a middle-sized university for the Deaf. (The rationale for the inclusion of White Deaf individuals as a cultural group but not African Americans who are deaf is provided in that chapter.) The Jamaican samples were drawn from two colleges in Jamaica; and the Japanese samples from a large university in Japan.

Jamaican culture was included for two reasons. First, almost no research on human communication processes has been conducted with this cultural group. Second, like other Caribbean cultures, Jamaican culture is an interesting blend—with African, British,

European, North American, Central American, South American, and Asian influences. Japanese culture was included because only one study has been conducted in this research tradition (Ju, in Nicotera and Associates 1993), which stopped at testing traditional attributes of the mate relationship. None of the propositions has been tested in Japanese culture.

This sampling is obviously not representative of the wide variety of cultural groups in the United States and internationally—and is not intended to be such. As a straight application and extension of the tradition, it was important to continue the work with college student populations. There is a great need for the inclusion of other U.S. cultural groups in this research tradition. There are practical problems in studying U.S. cultural groups while maintaining the college student population. Intact groups are not often readily available, and those that are available are usually racially, but not culturally, homogeneous. For example, sampling a Hispanic or Asian or Native American student organization would include individuals from a variety of specific cultures. This volume offers a start to the process of examining and comparing U.S. co-cultures, taking advantage of the existence of intact cultural groups that are both readily available and fairly culturally homogeneous. The groups studied do allow interesting comparisons. As stated in the preface to this volume, there is still much to be done in this line of work. This volume is merely the beginning of the theory's application cross-culturally.

Procedures

Nicotera and Associates (1993) demonstrated the set of techniques used here which both identifies relational stages and attributes in different cultures and allows for cross-cultural comparison without distortion. The method for level and attribute identification was twofold. First, open-ended surveys were distributed to samples in each culture. These surveys asked respondents to list attributes of the mate relationship. Then, respondents were asked to list the levels (stages) through which mate relationships progress from least to most intimate. The results of these questions were used to identify the most commonly mentioned attributes (RQ1a) and levels (RQ1b). (The specifics of these analyses are provided below under "analysis.") In this first stage of data collection, participants (except for those in Japan) were also asked to list several sources (topics) of conflict in mate relationships. As with attributes and levels, the most commonly mentioned of these were used to construct part of the second survey. Finally the surveys (except for Japan) asked respondents to list what makes for a high quality relationship (RQ5).

For the second stage of data collection, the selected labels for attributes and levels were arrayed in a questionnaire in paired comparisons of attributes with levels (RQ2); levels with the concept "ideal mate" and with the most intimate level (RQ1b); the concept "breaking up" with "lack of" each attribute (RQ3a); conflict sources with levels (RQ3b); and the concept "relationship quality" with "personal growth (generally)," "intimacy (generally)," personal growth in relation to each attribute in turn, and good communication about each attribute in turn (RQ4). Finally, following all the paired comparisons was a set of questions asking what "things could cause conflict" for each of the relationship stages (RQ3b). These second surveys were distributed to a second sample from each cultural population.

Analysis

The results of the first survey provided data that were analyzed to explore RQs 1a, 1b, and 5. RQs 1a and 1b assess the appropriate labels for attributes and levels of mate relationships in each culture. For each cultural group, if thirty percent or more of the sample listed an attribute, it was considered to be an important characteristic of the mate relationship for that culture. The resulting list of attributes represents the answer to RQ1a.

For the level designations (RQ1b), a qualitative analysis was employed. For each culture, a large set of stage lists was generated. These lists were examined for commonalities and patterns, and a general set of stages was generated. This general set of stages was then compared to each individual list and refined until it was judged that the general list was a fair representation of all individual lists. As a final caution, a research assistant compared each individual list against the general list to be sure the general list did not contradict any individual list. The general list represents the answer to RQ1b.

The second survey was generated and analyzed with the Galileo computer program. In this method, a set of concepts are arranged in all possible paired comparisons and participants are asked to estimate the "distances" between the concepts. Because a full Galileo model was not necessary for this research, all paired comparisons that were not relevant to the RQs were deleted. This helped to avoid the problem of participant fatigue due to the large number of concepts. In a full Galileo model, the aggregate configuration of concepts is factor analyzed, quantified, and verified with Galileo analysis. The Galileo computer program determines the uniqueness of dimensions and perceived social distance relative to a specific point of reference. Without a full set of paired-comparison data, the Galileo program cannot generate this full analysis. Instead, the program was used to generate means and z-scores (with outliers controlled for) to examine how the concepts in the survey relate to each other in each culture.

In the second survey, items from the lists of attributes and levels, as described above, were arranged in paired comparisons such that all the levels were paired with the concepts "ideal mate," "commitment," and with the most intimate level. The mean values of these distances were used to quantitatively verify the progression of stages generated qualitatively (RQ1b). In addition, z-scores of difference were computed (with outliers controlled for) so that all levels could be compared on their mean distances from the most intimate level, and from the concepts "ideal mate" and "commitment" (RQ1b). The results of these analyses allowed necessary adjustments to be made before analyzing data for RQ2.

The term "ideal mate" was used because this line of work has traditionally used it as the criterion for measuring increasing degrees of mateship (Cushman and Cahn 1985; Nicotera and Associates 1993). For these investigations, the term "commitment" was also used because the theoretic tradition has characterized the developing mate relationship in terms of increasing commitment. "A mate relationship grows more permanent as the couple achieves a deepening sense of *commitment*. The closer the other comes to one's ideal conception of a mate, the more likely one is to clear the field of competitors and feel *committed* to the relationship" (Cushman and Cahn, in Nicotera and Associates 1993, 140, [*emphasis mine*]). It is clear from this description that commitment is a concrete operationalization of the more abstract concept of the "ideal mate." To further illustrate this point, Cushman and Cahn (in Nicotera and Associates 1993) go on to describe attempts by researchers to discriminate between levels of mateship as attempts to "discriminate between different degrees or levels of developing *commitment*" (Cushman and Cahn, in Nicotera and Associates 1993, 140, [*emphasis mine*]).

Research Question 2 assesses which of the attributes generated by RQ1 are entry variables and which are intensity variables. The mean distances between the attributes and the levels were examined. Entry variables are those attributes whose mean distances to the levels remain the same across levels; intensity variables are those whose distances become progressively smaller as the level increases in intimacy. These progressions were statistically verified by the computation of z-scores of difference (with outliers controlled for) which reveal whether progressive relationship levels are significantly different in their respective mean distances from the attributes in question.

Research Question 3a assesses whether a lack of the attributes discovered in RQ1 is related to relational disintegration. To explore this RQ, mean distances and z-scores of difference (with outliers controlled for) between the "lack of" each attribute and the concept "breaking up" were examined. RQ3b seeks to identify sources of conflict for each level and for mate relationships in general. First, the list of conflict sources from the first survey were analyzed to create a list of those mentioned by at least thirty percent of the sample. Mean distances and z-scores of difference (with outliers controlled for) were examined between these conflict sources and the levels, as decided upon after quantitative analysis of Galileo data on levels. Finally, the open-ended question in the second survey elicited further sources, specific to each level.

Research Question 4 attempts to determine whether relational quality is linked to intimacy (generally), personal growth (generally), and to personal growth and good communication in regard to each attribute. To assess this question, mean distances and z-scores of difference (with outliers controlled for) are examined between the concept "quality relationship" and the following other concepts: intimacy (generally); personal growth (generally); personal growth in relation to each attribute in turn; and good communication about each attribute in turn. The final research question seeks to generate other factors that contribute to relationship quality. This question was assessed by examining lists generated in the first survey, as described above.

Summary and Organization of the Book

This chapter has given a brief overview of the prior progress made in this research program (Nicotera and Associates 1993), summarized the paradigmatic assumptions and the original general theory (Cushman and Cahn 1985; Cushman, Valentinsen, and Dietrich 1982), presented the RQs to be pursued in the research in this book, and described the general methodological procedures to be used to examine those RQs. Chapters Two through Six present studies in several cultures that examine RQs 1a, 1b, and 2. Data from White Americans, the traditional population for this line of research that studies "Americans," is presented in Chapter Two; data from African Americans in Chapter Three; from White Deaf Americans in Chapter Four; from Jamaicans in Chapter Five; and from Japanese in Chapter Six. Chapter Seven then presents the results of RQs 3a and 3b (regarding conflict and relational maintenance) for the American co-cultures and Jamaica. Chapter Eight presents the results of RQs 4 and 5 (regarding relationship quality) for the American co-cultures and Jamaica. The last chapter provides a discussion of cultural comparison, discusses the implications of this body of work, and looks to its future.

CHAPTER TWO

WHITE AMERICANS OF EUROPEAN DESCENT

Introduction

One of the great limitations in communication research is our traditional ethnocentric assumption that "White Euro-America" equals "America." Although cautions about generalizing from college student populations have long been heard in the field, little has been said about the invalidity of generalizing from *majority white* college students. In fact, until recently, racial or ethnic data were not routinely included in sample descriptions unless such data were explicitly analyzed as part of the study. Numerous recent works (i.e., Asante and Davis 1989; Collier 1988, 1991; Hecht, Collier, and Ribeau 1993; Hecht, Larkey, and Johnson 1992; Hecht and Ribeau 1984, 1987; Hecht, Ribeau, and Alberts 1989; Hecht, Ribeau, and Sedano, 1990; Keane-Dawes 1995; Martin, Hecht, and Larkey 1994; Shuter 1982) have made quite clear that in the U.S. population, rules and expectations for competent communication vary by co-culture.

The research tradition extended in the present body of work (see Nicotera and Associates 1993) has similarly failed to account for U.S. co-cultures. As stated in Chapter One, this may be why Nicotera (in Nicotera and Associates 1993) failed to find intracultural homogeneity for mateship levels in her U.S. sample. Although the U.S. samples in this research tradition have been majority white, these data are anecdotal; no racial or ethnic data were considered in these samples. Thus, the first task in refining this research is to clarify that what has been inappropriately called "U.S. culture" as "White-European U.S. culture" and to do so with data specifically from that population.

Research Questions

This chapter provides an investigation that examines Propositions 1 and 3 for White Americans of European descent. Proposition 1 states that perceived self-concept support is the basis of interpersonal attraction. As stated in Chapter One, two research questions were posed to discover the culturally-specific attributes and levels of mate relationships.

RQ1a: What are the attributes of mate relationships?

RQ1b: What are the levels of mate relationships?

Proposition 3 states that different types of self-concept support are the basis for *entry* into and increasing *intensity* of interpersonal relationships. The following research question was posed to discover the culture-specific nature of the attributes elicited by the pursuit of RQ1a, above.

RQ2:   Which attributes are entry and which are intensity variables?

Procedures

As described in Chapter One, the method for identification of attributes and levels was twofold. First, open-ended surveys were distributed. These surveys asked respondents to list attributes of the mate relationship. Then, respondents were asked to list the levels (stages) through which mate relationships progress from least to most intimate. The results of these questions were used to identify the most commonly mentioned attributes (RQ1a) and levels (RQ1b). In this first stage of data collection, participants were also asked several questions that were used to explore RQs 3, 4, and 5. Analyses of these data are presented in Chapters Seven and Eight.

For the second stage of data collection, the selected labels for attributes and levels were arrayed in a Galileo (see Chapter One) questionnaire in paired comparisons of attributes with levels (RQ2); levels with the concepts "ideal mate," "commitment," and with the most intimate level in the sequence (RQ1b). Several other paired comparisons were included for examination of RQs that are explored in Chapters Seven and Eight. This second survey was distributed to a second sample. Both surveys also included basic questions about demographics and relationship history. The answers to these basic questions were used for sample description.

Samples

The first survey was distributed to forty-two undergraduate students enrolled in a communication course at a large predominantly white university. In addition to white students of European descent, the respondents included ten individuals whose surveys were dropped from this analysis: four African Americans, one Hispanic, one Native American, one Asian American, one mixed race individual, and two international students. The surveys from African American students were subsequently included in the study of that group (Chapter Three).

The remaining sample for this study included fourteen males and eighteen females with an average age of twenty-one years. Regarding relational history, twenty-one respondents indicated that they were currently involved in a mate-type opposite sex relationship; one respondent was married, two were engaged, two were currently living with a boy/girlfriend, and one had cohabited in the past. All remaining participants indicated that they had been involved in mate-type opposite sex relationships in the past.

The second survey was distributed to thirty-five students enrolled in a communication course at the same university; twenty-eight responded. There was no overlap between the two samples. Three surveys had to be dropped from this analysis (two African Americans and one Hispanic). The remaining sample consisted of ten males and fifteen females, with an average age of twenty-two years. The majority of the sample (twenty-two) were single; one was married, one was engaged, and one was divorced. The remaining participants indicated that they were either currently or had in the past been involved in mate-type opposite sex relationships.

Results and Interpretation

Research question 1a. As described in Chapter One, the first research question, seeking to identify salient attributes of the mate relationship, was answered with responses to the question in the first survey that asked respondents to list at least ten "characteristics of a mate-type (dating, romantic) relationship." Table 2.1 contains these results.

Table 2.1   Mateship Attributes for White Americans of European Descent

ATTRIBUTE	% MALES	% FEMALES	% TOTAL
trust	57	72	66
friendship	50	56	53
love	50	56	53
honesty	43	56	50
communication	36	44	41
caring	36	28	31
loyalty	36	28	31
intimacy/closeness	43	17	28
sexual activity	36	22	28
attraction	14	33	25
humor	14	33	25
fidelity/faithful	36	17	25
togetherness	36	17	25
affection	14	22	19
phys. attractiveness	21	17	19
respect	7	22	16
companionship	7	22	16
intelligence	7	17	13
support	0	22	13
commitment	14	11	13
compatibility	14	11	13
interdependence	21	6	13
openness	7	17	13

physical affection	14	11	13
sacrifice	29	0	13
sharing	14	11	13
understnding	7	17	13
sexual attraction	14	6	9
argument	7	11	9
disclosure	14	6	9
fun	7	11	9
similar background	7	11	9
strong	0	17	9
admiration	7	6	6
dependable/responsible	14	0	6
friendly	7	6	6
happiness	7	6	6
interest	7	6	6
mutual interests	0	11	6
security	0	11	6
sensitive	14	0	6
similar views	0	11	6
sincerity	0	11	6
stable	7	6	6
warm	14	0	6

A total of eighty-six attributes were mentioned; forty-one of these were mentioned only once and are not included in the table. Of the forty-five attributes mentioned by more than one respondent, seven were mentioned by at least thirty percent of the sample. These are TRUST, FRIENDSHIP, LOVE, HONESTY, COMMUNICATION, CARING, and LOYALTY. These seven attributes were included in the second (Galileo) survey to assess their status as entry or intensity variables. In addition, several attributes that did not meet the thirty percent criterion were included in the second survey for their consideration regarding RQ2 (assessment as entry or intensity variables): AFFECTION, PHYSICAL ATTRACTIVENESS, RESPECT, INTELLIGENCE, SUPPORT, and SEXUAL ATTRACTION. All attributes considered in RQ2 are printed in boldface in Table 2.1.

In this research tradition (see Cushman and Cahn 1985 and Nicotera and Associates 1993), three entry variables (physical attractiveness, sexual appeal, and intelligence) and three intensity variables (affection, respect, and support) have been generally accepted for U.S. mate relationships. Because all six of these attributes appeared on the general list, they were also included on the second survey for assessment as regards RQ2.

Research Question 1b. As described in Chapter One, this research question, seeking to identify salient labels for increasing levels of the mate relationship, was answered with responses to the question in the first survey that asked respondents to "list the stages a mate-type (dating, romantic) relationship goes through as it progresses from least to most intimate." These data were subjected to a qualitative analysis. The lists were examined for commonalities and patterns, and a general set of stages was generated. This general set of stages was then compared to each individual list and refined until it was judged that the general list was a fair representation of all individual lists. As a final caution, a research assistant compared each individual list against the general list to be sure the general list did not contradict any individual list. The general list included the following levels, each subsequent level representing an increase in intimacy: OCCASIONAL DATE, REGULAR DATE, EXCLUSIVE DATE, SEXUAL PARTNER, COHABITATION, and MARRIAGE.

This list of stages was then subjected to a quantitative analysis using the second (Galileo) survey. The paired comparisons in the Galileo survey included the concepts "ideal mate" and "commitment" (the latter coincidentally also appeared on the list of attributes, but did not meet the thirty percent criterion) paired with each

Table 2.2 Mateship Levels for White Americans of European Descent

	IDEAL MATE	COMMITMENT
OCCASIONAL DATE	103.5	92.12
REGULAR DATE	42.42	69.84
EXCLUSIVE DATE	36.42	46.64
SEXUAL PARTNERS	31.16	38.79
COHABITATION	24.75	25.80
MARRIAGE	9.72	5.08

relationship level. The mean values of these distances were used to quantitatively verify the progression of stages generated qualitatively. These results are presented in Table 2.2. The table shows that the mean distances from each indicator of intimacy (ideal mate and commitment) do indeed decrease as the level designation increases. The sequence of levels does depict increasing levels of mateship intimacy.

In addition to the analysis of mean distances from ideal mate and commitment, z-scores of difference were computed so that all level designations were compared on their mean distances from the most intimate level (MARRIAGE) and from the concepts COMMITMENT and IDEAL MATE. These results are presented in Tables 2.3 and 2.4.

Table 2.3 Z-scores of Difference Between Mateship Levels on Distance From Most Intimate Level: White Americans of European Descent

	OCCASIONAL DATE	REGULAR DATE	EXCLUSIVE DATE	SEXUAL PARTNER	COHABITATION
REGULAR DATE	0.38				
EXCLUSIVE DATE	2.02*	1.53			
SEXUAL PARTNER	2.77*	2.29*	2.39*		
COHABITATION	3.16*	2.68*	3.86*	1.60	
MARRIAGE	3.63*	3.15*	6.24*	4.42*	2.89*

*p<.05

The labels for mateship levels are, in sequence, OCCASIONAL DATE, REGULAR DATE, EXCLUSIVE DATE, SEXUAL PARTNER, COHABITATION, and MARRIAGE. The z-scores of difference in Table 2.3 represent the differences between the mean distances of each level from the top end of the scale (MARRIAGE); for example the figure .38, between OCCASIONAL DATE and REGULAR DATE, represents the z-score of the difference between the mean distance of OCCASIONAL DATE with MARRIAGE and the mean distance of REGULAR DATE with MARRIAGE. As shown in Table 2.3, REGULAR DATE is not significantly closer to marriage than OCCASIONAL DATE, the previous level in the sequence. However, the next level, EXCLUSIVE DATE, is significantly closer to MARRIAGE than is OCCASIONAL DATE. Because EXCLUSIVE DATE is not significantly closer to MARRIAGE than is REGULAR DATE, REGULAR DATE was dropped from the sequence for subsequent analysis.

Moving on in the sequence, the step from EXCLUSIVE DATE to SEXUAL PARTNER is significant. However, COHABITATION is not significantly closer to MARRIAGE than is SEXUAL PARTNER, although COHABITATION is significantly different from MARRIAGE—the distance between COHABITATION and MARRIAGE being significantly greater than the distance between MARRIAGE and itself (zero). COHABITATION was dropped from the sequence for subsequent analysis. (SEXUAL PARTNER is also significantly different from MARRIAGE.) Although the sequence of labels does represent increasing levels of ideal mateness and commitment, as shown in Table 2.2, not every step in the sequence is a statistically significantly different degree of mateness.

The statistical significance of the levels as different designations of increasing levels of mateship was further investigated by examining the differences between the levels regarding their mean distances from COMMITMENT and IDEAL MATE. Table 2.4 presents these results.

Table 2.4 Z-scores of Difference Between Mateship Levels on Distances From Commitment and Ideal Mate: White Americans of European Descent

	OCCASIONAL DATE	REGULAR DATE	EXCLUSIVE DATE	SEXUAL PARTNER	COHABITATION	MARRIAGE
OCCASIONAL DATE		1.33	2.93*	3.46*	4.53*	6.85*
REGULAR DATE	1.46		1.55	2.10*	3.14*	5.41*
EXCLUSIVE DATE	1.61	0.58		0.58	1.66	4.07*
SEXUAL PARTNER	1.73	1.08	0.50		1.05	3.36*
COHABITATION	1.89	1.73	1.14	0.62		2.36*
MARRIAGE	2.27*	3.74*	3.05*	2.41*	1.74	

upper triangle= COMMITMENT
lower triangle= IDEAL MATE
*p<.05

Table 2.4 shows that OCCASIONAL DATE and REGULAR DATE do not represent significantly different concepts in relation to either COMMITMENT or IDEAL MATE. The next step in the sequence is also not significant. REGULAR DATE and EXCLUSIVE DATE are not significantly different in their respective distances from COMMITMENT and IDEAL MATE. The decision to drop REGULAR DATE from the sequence was thus substantiated. EXCLUSIVE DATE is significantly closer than OCCASIONAL DATE to COMMITMENT but not to IDEAL MATE.

Moving on in the sequence, EXCLUSIVE DATE is not significantly different from SEXUAL PARTNER nor from COHABITATION in their respective distances from COMMITMENT and IDEAL MATE. However, EXCLUSIVE DATE and MARRIAGE are significantly different in their respective distances from both COMMITMENT and IDEAL MATE. The decision to drop COHABITATION from the sequence was thus substantiated. Furthermore, these results provide evidence to warrant dropping SEXUAL PARTNER as well, since it seems to be redundant with EXCLUSIVE DATE in terms of both degree of commitment and level of ideal mateness.

The resulting sequence consists of three levels, OCCASIONAL DATE, EXCLUSIVE DATE, and MARRIAGE. Although the first step in sequence does not represent a significant increase in the degree of ideal mateness, the second step does. Each step in this sequence represents a significant increase in the degree of commitment, which is a concrete operationalization of the more abstract term "ideal mate" (see Chapter One). Most importantly, as shown in Table 2.3, each subsequent level is significantly closer to the most intimate level.

Research Question 2. As explained in Chapter One, this RQ asks which mateship variables operate as entry variables and which as intensity variables. The mean distances between the attributes (identified in analysis for RQ1a—TRUST, FRIENDSHIP, LOVE, HONESTY, COMMUNICATION, CARING, LOYALTY, AFFECTION, PHYSICAL ATTRACTIVENESS, RESPECT, INTELLIGENCE, SUPPORT, and SEXUAL ATTRACTION) and the levels OCCASIONAL DATE, EXCLUSIVE DATE, and MARRIAGE were examined. Entry variables are those attributes whose mean distances to the levels remain stable across levels; intensity variables are those whose mean distances become progressively smaller as the levels increase in intimacy. These progressions were statistically verified by the computation of z-scores of difference which

Table 2.5   Mean Distances Between Attributes and Levels: White Americans of European Descent

	OCCASIONAL DATE	EXCLUSIVE DATE	MARRIAGE
trust	73.76	33.40	2.52
friendship	46.92	26.28	11.32
love	84.72	81.18	5.56
honesty	67.00	26.92	5.52
communication	47.76	17.63	11.96
caring	54.60	27.88	7.60
loyalty	75.60	28.96	16.20
phys. attractiveness	50.50	30.50	29.38
sexual attraction	48.12	26.96	17.00
intelligence	64.16	32.72	14.40
respect	29.76	18.88	11.40
support	69.83	34.46	9.12
affection	52.88	25.04	5.84

reveal whether progressive relationship levels are significantly different in their respective mean distances from the attributes in question.

Table 2.5 shows that all the attributes are progressively closer to more intimate mateship levels, indicating that each is an important characteristic of the mate relationship. The more important analysis, however, appears in Table 2.6, which shows whether these mean distances become significantly closer to higher mateship levels. Those that do not can be labeled entry variables; those that do can be labeled intensity variables. The z-scores in Table 2.6 indicate that three attributes are neither significantly closer to EXCLUSIVE DATE than to OCCASIONAL DATE, nor are they significantly closer to MARRIAGE than to EXCLUSIVE DATE. Hence, these three attributes operate as entry variables: FRIENDSHIP, PHYSICAL ATTRACTIVENESS, and RESPECT. Six attributes are significantly closer to EXCLUSIVE DATE than to OCCASIONAL DATE, and are also significantly closer to MARRIAGE than to EXCLUSIVE DATE. Hence, these six attrib-

Table 2.6 Z-scores of Difference Between Subsequent Levels on
Distances From Attributes: White Americans of European Descent

	OCCASIONAL DATE and EXCLUSIVE DATE	EXCLUSIVE DATE and MARRIAGE
trust	3.37*	4.09*
friendship	1.58	1.78
love	0.15	3.47*
honesty	3.73*	3.28*
communication	3.27*	0.78
caring	2.68*	2.92*
loyalty	4.07*	1.42
phys. attractiveness	1.88	0.12
sexual attraction	1.96*	1.09
intelligence	2.65*	2.42*
respect	1.15	0.94
support	2.43*	2.81*
affection	2.80*	3.01*

*p<.05

utes operate as intensity variables: TRUST, HONESTY, CARING, INTEL-
LIGENCE, SUPPORT, and AFFECTION.

The remaining four attributes are significant at one step in the
sequence of levels, but not at the other. To meaningfully interpret
the operation of these variables, we must consider the nature of the
transition between the mateship levels. The transition between
OCCASIONAL DATE and EXCLUSIVE DATE is one of what Cushman and
Cahn (1985) call "clearing the field" of competitors. It is at this
juncture that the pair becomes a couple. The transition between
EXCLUSIVE DATE and MARRIAGE is one of making a formal binding
commitment. It is at this juncture that the couple has formally
and publicly declared an intent to permanently commit to one
another as mates.

LOVE is not significantly closer to EXCLUSIVE DATE than to OCCA-
SIONAL DATE, but it is significantly closer to MARRIAGE. The juncture

at which LOVE becomes significantly closer is the point of formal public declaration of commitment to one another as mates. Apparently, love need not increase in the relationship for a clearing of the field to occur, but must increase greatly for a formal commitment to be made. Given the small difference between the means at the first juncture and the enormous difference at the second (see Table 2.5), the role of love in this second transition is apparently quite salient and important. Love cannot be considered an intensity variable in the sense in which such variables have been conceptually defined for this study. However, since an increase in love is clearly a crucial requirement for the relationship to progress to a full mateship commitment, it must be judged to operate similarly. Hence, it will be labeled a commitment-intensity variable.

COMMUNICATION, LOYALTY, and SEXUAL ATTRACTION operate differently. These attributes are significantly closer to EXCLUSIVE DATE than to OCCASIONAL DATE, but are not significantly closer to MARRIAGE. The juncture at which these attributes become significantly closer is the point of "clearing the field." Unlike LOVE, which need not increase for the field to be cleared, COMMUNICATION, LOYALTY, and SEXUAL ATTRACTION are salient at this juncture. Once the field has been cleared, COMMUNICATION, LOYALTY, and SEXUAL ATTRACTION operate similarly to entry variables. These variables might be labeled "marker" variables, since they seem to mark the point at which the pair clears the field to become a couple.

Conclusions

The list of attributes generated by the open-ended survey is consistent with the literature on mate relationships. For European Americans, a mate relationship is characterized by trust, friendship, love, honesty, communication, caring, and loyalty. Although of lesser salience to the sample in this study, the relationship is also characterized by perceptions of physical attraction, sexual attraction, intelligence, respect, support, and affection. This second list has been traditionally thought to include the crucial attributes for "U.S. culture" (see Nicotera and Associates 1993). The fact that none of these attributes passed the thirty percent criterion is an important indicator of the dangers of assuming generalizations across U.S. populations, across co-cultures, and across time. However, at the same time, the fact that all six did appear confirms the validity of past research. The power of these thirteen attributes in addressing relational maintenance and quality are addressed in Chapters Seven and Eight.

The mateship levels that were identified in this study are similar in character but different in semantic content from past research in this tradition. Qualitatively, the mate relationship progresses through the following stages: occasional date, regular date, exclusive date, sexual partner, cohabitation, and marriage, each level representing a quantitatively greater degree of commitment. Statistical analysis showed, however, that these seven stages are somewhat redundant. By analyzing significant differences between subsequent stages, the list was reduced to three necessary stages. In comparison to past research, this set of three stages—occasional date, exclusive date, and marriage—though semantically different, is functionally strikingly similar to the sequence that has traditionally been accepted in this line of work (casual date, steady date, fiancee, and spouse), but for which Nicotera (in Nicotera and Associates 1993) failed to find support. Hence, the seminal work in this research tradition is substantiated as having identified a functionally stable set of stages for White European U.S. culture. It may be that the semantic difference in the labels for levels in this study is due to the refinement of specifically targeting White Americans of European descent, rather than the ambiguous and falsely assumed existence of a generalized "U.S. culture." As will be noted from Chapters Three and Four, data from other co-cultural groups in the United States reveal sets of stages that are functionally similar but different in important ways.

The one functional difference between the traditional labels (casual date, steady date, fiancee, and spouse) and the labels found in this study is that data from this study did not specify a stage that is a precursor to marriage. However, "engaged" was mentioned as a stage by three of the thirty-two respondents to the open-ended survey. Because it was so infrequently mentioned, it was decided that it was not representative of the sample's lists. However, hindsight reveals that "engaged" might well have found significance as a functional mateship stage had it been included as a concept in the Galileo survey. The concepts "sexual partner" and "cohabitation" were mentioned with greater frequency, yet failed to represent necessary, nonredundant stages. Perhaps the assumption that frequency of mention of stages is an indication of the uniqueness and necessity of a stage was unfounded. It may be that participants who mentioned marriage but not engagement did so because in their judgment, marriage presumes an engagement phase.

The nature of the attributes as entry or intensity variables is another area that only partially supports the past research in this tradition. Of the three traditionally accepted entry variables (physical attractiveness, sexual attraction, and intelligence), only one was found in this study to operate as an entry variable. Physical attractiveness does not differ in its distance from the mateship levels. Self-concept support of the other on physical attractiveness need not increase for the relationship to develop. Sexual attraction was labeled a marker variable in this study. Self-concept support of the other on sexual attraction does need to increase for the pair to clear the field. However, once the field is cleared, the variable operates similarly to physical attractiveness. The pair need not increase their self-concept support for each other on sexual attraction for the relationship to develop further. Finally, intelligence operates as an intensity variable in this study. In order for the relationship to progress to subsequent stages, self-concept support of intelligence must increase at each stage. This is directly contradictory of past research. This may indicate the importance of specifying the culture rather than assuming a generalizable "U.S. culture." It may also signify an important difference in values between college students of the 1990s and those of previous generations.

The traditionally accepted intensity variables are respect, support, and affection. Again, this study only partially supports the traditional research findings. Support and affection operate as intensity variables; progression to deeper stages of intimacy require that these variables increase. However, respect operates as an entry variable; it need not increase for the relationship to deepen.

Turning to the seven variables revealed in this study, an additional entry variable, friendship, was identified. This indicates an important cultural value that the mate relationship is first a friendship. Before embarking on a mate relationship, the pair must feel they have established a friendship. Three intensity variables were also identified: trust, honesty, and caring. Self-concept support on these variables must continually increase for the pair to progress to deeper intimacy and commitment. Love, on the other hand, need increase only after the field has been cleared, reflecting the newly-coined phrase "commitment-intensity variable." Finally, communication and loyalty operate in the same way as sexual attraction; they have also been labeled marker variables. Self-concept support of the other on communication and loyalty does need to increase for the pair to clear the field. However, once the field is cleared, the variables operate similarly to entry variables. The pair need not increase their self-concept support for each other on these variables for the relationship to develop beyond the exclusive date phase.

This study has revealed different results from the traditional research in this tradition, only partially supporting past findings. The general theoretic structure is supported, however, and the general methodology has been once again shown to be fruitful. The importance of this study is the cultural refinement. No longer can we be comfortable in our Eurocentric assumption that there is one American culture. By specifically focusing on White Americans of European descent, this study has improved upon the past research which blindly studied that general population without controlling for cultural variations within samples. Although we know anecdotally that the "American" samples in this research tradition were predominantly white, we do not know how much precision was lost to such within-sample variation. The subsequent chapters seek to further refine our understanding of the general multi-cultural U.S. population.

CHAPTER THREE

AFRICAN AMERICANS

Introduction

Communication researchers' traditional ethnocentric bias that "White Euro-America" equals "America" is grounded in a Eurocentric bias. In recent years, attention to African American populations has been growing in the field of interpersonal communication. In particular, researchers have identified cultural values, norms, and social conventions that impact African American communication both intra- and interculturally. Kochman (1982), for example, describes generally divergent patterns of intonation, spontaneity, aggressiveness, and argument between African American and European American cultures. LaFrance and Mayo (1976) had earlier demonstrated that eye gaze differed between African American and European American cultures; African Americans tend to maintain eye contact while speaking, European Americans while listening. More germane to the topic at hand, Hecht and Ribeau (1984) specify features of interaction that African American communicators find satisfying: a focus on intimate topical involvement, trust, and other orientation.

Martin, Hecht, and Larkey (1994) summarize this literature in a set of five core values for African American culture that "represent a constellation of meaning and interpretations that frame a group's understanding of the world and guide social behavior" (237). These values are sharing, uniqueness, positivity, realism, and assertiveness (Hecht, Collier, and Ribeau 1993; Rose 1982/3; White and Parham 1990). *Sharing* endorses the group and can be

35

summarized as a reflection of collectivism (Hofstede 1980). The central unifying concepts represented in the value of sharing are interconnectedness, interrelatedness, and interdependence (Rose 1982/3; White and Parham, 1990). *Uniqueness* pays homage to the individual. "African Americans try to demonstrate both individuality and commonality in interactions with others" (Martin *et al.* 1994, 237, citing Rose 1982/3).

Positivism denotes a sense of "aliveness, emotional vitality and openness of feelings, and being resilient" (237) in this positivism which is strongly grounded in *realism*, described as "understanding and communicating both the positive *and* negative in the world" (237)—in the vernacular, "tellin' it like it is" (237). Finally, *assertiveness* is valued as the individual is expected to take charge of her/his own existence and stand up for her/himself in the face of oppression (Jenkins 1982).

In a study that highlights the questionable validity of generalizing interpersonal communication theory across American co-cultures, Gudykunst and Hammer (1987) report that for African American communicators uncertainty reduction does not necessarily lead to liking and that interrogation does not reduce uncertainty. The literature clearly demonstrates not only that findings from communication studies of European Americans cannot be validly generalized to African Americans, but that interpersonal communication theory may well be less universal in its explanations than we have assumed.

One of the first steps to correcting our Eurocentric bias in the field is to explore a variety of U.S. co-cultures, testing theories that have previously been assumed universal. The study presented in this chapter tests in an African American population the basic theoretic conception of relational development based on self-concept support for crucial relationship attributes.

Research Questions

This chapter provides an investigation that examines Propositions 1 and 3 for African Americans. Proposition 1 states that perceived self-concept support is the basis of interpersonal attraction. As stated in Chapter One, two research questions were posed to discover the culturally-specific attributes and levels of mate relationships.

    RQ1a: What are the attributes of mate relationships?

    RQ1b: What are the levels of mate relationships?

Proposition 3 states that different types of self-concept support are the bases for *entry* into and increasing *intensity* of interpersonal relationships. The following research question was posed to discover the culture-specific nature of the attributes elicited by the pursuit of RQ1a, above.

    RQ2:   Which attributes are entry and which are intensity variables?

Procedures

As described in Chapter One, the method for identification of attributes and levels was twofold. First, open-ended surveys were distributed. These surveys asked respondents to list attributes of the mate relationship. Then, respondents were asked to list the levels (stages) through which mate relationships progress from least to most intimate. The results of these questions were used to identify the most commonly mentioned attributes (RQ1a) and levels (RQ1b). In this first stage of data collection, participants were also asked several questions which were used to explore RQs 3, 4, and 5. Analyses of these data are presented in Chapters Seven and Eight.

For the second stage of data collection, the selected labels for attributes and levels were arrayed in a Galileo (see Chapter One) questionnaire in paired comparisons of attributes with levels (RQ2); levels with the concepts "ideal mate," "commitment," and with the most intimate level in the sequence (RQ1b). Several other paired comparisons were included for examination of RQs that are explored in Chapters Seven and Eight. This second survey was distributed to a second sample. Both surveys also included basic questions about demographics and relationship history. The answers to these basic questions were used for sample description.

Samples

The first survey was distributed to twenty-five undergraduate students enrolled in a communication course at a middle-sized Historically Black university (HBU). In addition to African American students, the respondents included six individuals whose surveys were dropped from this analysis (five African Caribbeans and one mixed race individual). The remaining sample for this study included six males and thirteen females with an average age of nineteen years. Regarding relational history, seventeen respondents indicated that they were currently involved in a mate-type opposite sex relationship; one respondent was married, one was engaged, and one was currently living with a boy/girlfriend. All participants indicated that they had been involved in mate-type opposite sex relationships in the past.

The second survey was distributed to fifty-one students enrolled in a communication course at the same university. There was no overlap between the two samples. Nine surveys had to be dropped from this analysis (five African Caribbeans, one African Hispanic, two mixed race individuals, and one international student). The remaining sample consisted of eighteen males and twenty-four females, with an average age of twenty years. All but one member of the sample were single; one was married, two were engaged. The remaining participants indicated that they were either currently or had in the past been involved in mate-type opposite sex relationships.

Results and Interpretation

Research Question 1a. As described in Chapter One, the first research question, seeking to identify salient attributes of the mate relationship, was answered with responses to the question in the first survey that asked respondents to list at least ten "characteristics of a mate-type (dating, romantic) relationship." Table 3.1 contains these results.

A total of seventy-eight attributes were mentioned; forty-seven of these were mentioned only once and are not included in the table. Of the thirty-one attributes mentioned by more than one

Table 3.1 Mateship Attributes for African Americans

ATTRIBUTE	% MALES	% FEMALES	% TOTAL
honesty	50	46	47
communication	17	54	42
love	17	54	42
caring	17	38	32
patient	33	31	32
trust	33	31	32
understanding	33	31	32
intelligent	17	23	21
respect	17	23	21
compatible	17	23	21
physically attractive	17	15	16
sexually appealing	0	23	16
commitment	0	23	16
educated	17	15	16
fidelity	17	15	16
friendship	0	23	16
romance	17	15	16
sharing	17	15	16
humor	0	23	16
affection	17	8	11
support	17	8	11
ambitious	17	8	11
considerate	0	15	11
family man	0	15	11
fun	17	8	11
goal oriented	0	15	11
independent	0	15	11
open-minded	0	15	11
spiritual	0	15	11
strong	17	8	11
talking	0	15	11

respondent, seven were mentioned by at least thirty percent of the sample. These are HONESTY, COMMUNICATION, LOVE, CARING, PATIENCE, TRUST, and UNDERSTANDING. These seven attributes were included in the second (Galileo) survey to assess their status as entry or intensity variables. In addition, several attributes that did not meet the thirty percent criterion were included in the second survey for their consideration regarding RQ2 (assessment as entry or intensity variables): INTELLIGENT, RESPECT, PHYSICALLY ATTRACTIVE, SEXUALLY APPEALING, AFFECTION, and SUPPORT. All attributes considered in RQ2 are printed in boldface in Table 3.1.

In this research tradition (see Cushman and Cahn 1985 and Nicotera and Associates 1993), three entry variables (physical attractiveness, sexual appeal, and intelligence) and three intensity variables (affection, respect, and support) have been generally accepted for U.S. mate relationships. Because all six of these attributes appeared on the general list, they were also included on the second survey for assessment as regards RQ2.

Research Question 1b. As described in Chapter One, this research question, seeking to identify salient labels for increasing levels of the mate relationship, was answered with responses to the question in the first survey that asked respondents to "list the stages a mate-type (dating, romantic) relationship goes through as it progresses from least to most intimate." These data were subjected to a qualitative analysis. The lists were examined for commonalities and patterns, and a general set of stages was generated. This general set of stages was then compared to each individual list and refined until it was judged that the general list was a fair representation of all individual lists. As a final caution, a research assistant compared each individual list against the general list to be sure the general list did not contradict any individual list. The general list included the following levels, each subsequent level representing an increase in intimacy: DATING, BEST FRIEND, LOVER, ENGAGED, and MARRIAGE.

This list of stages was then subjected to a quantitative analysis using the second (Galileo) survey. The paired comparisons in the Galileo survey included the concepts "ideal mate" and "commitment" (as in the White American study, the latter coincidentally also appeared on the list of attributes, but did not meet the thirty percent criterion) paired with each relationship level. The mean values of these distances were used to quantitatively verify the progression of stages generated qualitatively. These results are presented in Table 3.2. The table shows that the mean distances from each indicator of intimacy (ideal mate and commitment) do indeed decrease as the level designation increases, with the exception of BEST FRIEND and the step from ENGAGED to MARRIAGE for COMMITMENT. Without BEST FRIEND, the sequence of levels does generally depict increasing levels of mateship intimacy.

Table 3.2 Mateship Levels for African Americans

	IDEAL MATE	COMMITMENT
DATING	60.31	125.74
BEST FRIEND	473.17	34.24
LOVER	41.07	74.52
ENGAGED	21.77	8.00
MARRIAGE	21.56	16.69

In addition to the analysis of mean distances from ideal mate and commitment, z-scores of difference were computed so that all level designations were compared on their mean distances from the most intimate level (MARRIAGE) and from the concepts COMMITMENT and IDEAL MATE. These results are presented in Tables 3.3 and 3.4.

The labels for mateship levels are, in sequence, DATING, BEST FRIEND, LOVER, ENGAGED, and MARRIAGE. The z-scores of difference in Table 3.3 represent the differences between the mean distances of each level from the top end of the scale (MARRIAGE); for example the figure 2.65, between DATING and BEST FRIEND, represents the z-score of the difference between the mean distance of DATING from MARRIAGE and the mean distance of BEST FRIEND from MARRIAGE. As shown in Table 3.3, BEST FRIEND is significantly closer to MARRIAGE than DATING, the previous level in the sequence. However, neither of the next two levels, LOVER or ENGAGED, is sig-

Table 3.3 Z-scores of Difference Between Mateship Levels
on Distances From Most Intimate Level: African Americans

	DATING	BEST FRIEND	LOVER	ENGAGED
BEST FRIEND	2.65*			
LOVER	2.83*	0.59		
ENGAGED	2.90*	0.85	0.27	
MARRIAGE	3.65*	4.49*	4.34*	4.14*

*p<.05

nificantly different closer to MARRIAGE than is BEST FRIEND. Given the results for BEST FRIEND in Table 3.2, this level was dropped from the sequence for subsequent analysis.

Moving on through the sequence without BEST FRIEND, LOVER is significantly closer to MARRIAGE than is the previous level, DATING. However, ENGAGED is not significantly closer to MARRIAGE than is LOVER. LOVER was also dropped from the sequence for subsequent analysis. MARRIAGE is significantly different from all the other levels—the distance between each level and MARRIAGE being significantly greater than the distance between MARRIAGE and itself (zero). Although the sequence of labels does represent increasing levels of ideal mateness and commitment, as shown in Table 3.2 (with the exception of BEST FRIEND), not every step in the sequence is a statistically significantly different degree of mateness.

The statistical significance of the levels as different designations of increasing levels of mateship was further investigated by examining the differences between the levels regarding their mean distances from COMMITMENT and IDEAL MATE. Table 3.4 presents these results.

Table 3.4   Z-scores of Difference Between Mateship Levels on Distances
From Commitment and Ideal Mate: African Americans

	DATING	BEST FRIEND	LOVER	ENGAGED	MARRIAGE
DATING		2.62*	1.22	3.44*	3.65*
BEST FRIEND	0.98		1.55	3.14*	1.22
LOVER	0.85	0.99		2.65*	2.09*
ENGAGED	2.00*	0.99	1.32		0.68
MARRIAGE	1.96*	0.99	1.27	0.02	

upper triangle=COMMITMENT
lower triangle=IDEAL MATE
*p<.05

Table 3.4 shows that DATING and BEST FRIEND represent significantly different concepts in relation to COMMITMENT but not in relation
to IDEAL MATE. The next step in the sequence is also not significant.
BEST FRIEND and LOVER are not significantly different in their
respective distances from COMMITMENT and IDEAL MATE. Further,
LOVER and ENGAGED differ in relation to COMMITMENT but not IDEAL
MATE. The decision to drop BEST FRIEND and LOVER from the
sequence was thus substantiated.

DATING and ENGAGED are significantly different for both COMMIT-
MENT and IDEAL MATE. Finally, ENGAGED and MARRIAGE are not significantly different for either COMMITMENT or IDEAL MATE. It was
decided to retain only two levels (DATING and ENGAGED) because of
the results in Table 3.2 and because MARRIAGE was not a significantly different level of commitment, which is the crucial determi-
nant of increasing mateship intimacy.

Research Question 2. As explained in Chapter One, this RQ asks
which mateship variables operate as entry variables and which as
intensity variables. The mean distances between the attributes
(identified in analysis for RQ1a—HONESTY, COMMUNICATION, LOVE,

CARING, PATIENCE, TRUST, UNDERSTANDING, INTELLIGENT, RESPECT, PHYSICALLY ATTRACTIVE, SEXUALLY APPEALING, AFFECTION, and SUPPORT) and the levels DATING and ENGAGED were examined. Entry variables are those attributes whose mean distances to the levels remain stable across levels; intensity variables are those whose mean distances become progressively smaller as the levels increase in intimacy. These progressions were statistically verified by the computation of z-scores of difference, which reveal whether progressive relationship levels are significantly different in their respective mean distances from the attributes in question.

Table 3.5 Mean Distances Between Attributes and Levels: African Americans

ATTRIBUTE	DATING	ENGAGED	MARRIAGE
honesty	47.26	16.83	17.98
communication	36.22	12.88	16.80
love	131.86	10.29	22.02
caring	62.48	10.14	18.17
patient	74.57	29.81	31.05
trust	61.71	9.22	15.79
understanding	68.95	12.27	19.31
intelligent	129.56	70.24	79.25
respect	21.50	6.74	26.86
physically attractive	79.17	76.86	78.31
sexually appealing	72.36	27.08	37.10
affection	56.26	10.82	19.17
support	123.98	11.14	16.57

Table 3.5 shows that all the attributes are progressively closer to the more intimate mateship level, indicating that each is an important characteristic of the mate relationship. The more important analysis, however, appears in Table 3.6, which shows whether the mean distances in Table 3.5 become significantly closer to the high-

Table 3.6 Z-scores of Difference Between Subsequent Levels
on Distances From Attributes: African Americans

	DATING and ENGAGED	ENGAGED and MARRIAGE
honesty	3.14*	0.09
communication	3.38*	0.3
love	3.60*	0.86
caring	3.93*	0.61
patient	2.92*	0.08
trust	3.88*	0.52
understanding	3.81*	0.55
intelligent	1.29	0.24
respect	2.46*	0.83
physically attractive	0.06	0.04
sexually appealing	1.94	0.62
affection	4.69*	0.64
support	3.33*	0.43

*p<.05

er mateship level. Those that do not can be labeled entry variables; those that do can be labeled intensity variables. The z-scores in Table 3.6 indicate that three attributes are not significantly closer to ENGAGED than to DATING. Hence, these three attributes operate as entry variables: PHYSICALLY ATTRACTIVE, SEXUALLY APPEALING, and INTELLIGENT. These are the three traditionally assumed mateship entry variables (see Nicotera and Associates 1993).

The rest of the attributes are significantly closer to ENGAGED than to DATING. Hence, these ten attributes operate as intensity variables: HONESTY, COMMUNICATION, LOVE, CARING, PATIENCE, TRUST, UNDERSTANDING, RESPECT, AFFECTION, and SUPPORT. The last three are the traditional intensity variables identified in past work (see Nicotera and Associates 1993).

Conclusion

Like the results for White Americans of European descent, the list of attributes generated in this study is consistent with the literature on mate relationships. In African American culture, a mate relationship is characterized by honesty, communication, love, caring, patience, trust, and understanding. Although of lesser salience to the sample in this study, the relationship is also characterized by perceptions of intelligence, physical attraction, sexual appeal, respect, affection, and support. This second list has been traditionally thought to include the crucial attributes for "U.S. culture" (see Nicotera and Associates 1993). As for the White American sample, the fact that none of these attributes passed the thirty percent criterion is an important indicator of the dangers of assuming generalizations across U.S. populations, across co-cultures, and across time. However, at the same time, the fact that all six did appear confirms to some extent the validity of past research. The power of the attributes in addressing relational quality and maintenance are addressed in Chapters Seven and Eight.

The mateship levels that were identified in this study are somewhat different in both semantic content and function from past research in this tradition. Qualitatively, the mate relationship progresses through the following stages: dating, best friend, lover, engaged, and marriage, each level representing a quantitatively greater degree of commitment. In comparison to past research, this set of stages, though semantically different, is somewhat similar to the sequence that has traditionally been accepted in this line of work (casual date, steady date, fiancee, and spouse). However, it is not as similar as the sequence generated for European Americans (see Chapter Two). The idea of "best friend" and "lover" as levels of mateship progression add nuances that seem to reflect the cultural value of collectivity through sharing, interdependence, and openness of feelings.

Statistical analysis showed, however, that the stages found are functionally redundant in terms of commitment. By analyzing significant differences in commitment between subsequent stages, the list was reduced to only two necessary stages of commitment increase; this represents the important functional difference between the traditional labels (casual date, steady date, fiancee, and spouse) and the labels found in this study. The nature of the attributes as entry or intensity variables, however, supports the past research in this tradition. All three traditionally accepted entry variables (intelligence, physical attractiveness, and sexual appeal) were found to operate as entry variables. Self-concept support of the other on these variables need not increase for the relationship to develop. For the European American sample only one of these, physical attractiveness, operates as an entry variable; intelligence is an intensity variable; and sexual attraction is a marker variable (becoming stable across latter growth transitions).

The traditionally accepted intensity variables are respect, support, and affection. Again, this study supports the traditional research findings. All three operate as intensity variables; progression to deeper stages of intimacy require that these variables increase. For the European American sample, respect is an entry variable. Clearly, African American and European American samples differ significantly in the ways that these traditional variables operate.

The remaining variables revealed in this study (honesty, communication, love, caring, patience, trust, and understanding), were all identified as intensity variables. Self-concept support on these variables must continually increase for the pair to progress to deeper intimacy and commitment. For the European American sample, honesty, caring, and trust operate in the same way. However, love operates somewhat differently—perhaps owing to the fact that the European American data shows three stages rather than two, with love remaining stable across the first relational transition but increasing across the second. Communication operates for European Americans as a marker variable. The European American sample also did not mention patience or understanding as crucial attributes of the mate relationship. Conversely, the African American sample did not mention friendship or loyalty as relationship attributes.

This study has revealed different results from the traditional research in this tradition, supporting past findings for attributes but not for functional mateship levels as markers of significantly increasing commitment. The general theoretic structure is supported, however, and the general methodology has been once again shown to be fruitful. The importance of this study is the cultural refinement. No longer can we be comfortable in our Eurocentric assumption that there is one American culture.

Clearly, African Americans and European Americans differ in their intra-cultural progressions through mateship stages. Most striking is the discovery of only two statistically significant semantic markers for increasing commitment for African American culture. This finding is enriched by a consideration of the core cultural values reviewed by Martin *et al.* (1994). The value of *sharing* emphasizes emotional bonding. The point at which the relationship becomes committed is quite distinct, as compared to the more gradual process seen for European Americans. This may reflect the fact that emotional bonding is a core value of the culture and is thus revealed as the only important functional step in relational progression. In addition, this reflects the cultural value of *positivism*. There is a certain optimism reflected in the process of seeking interdependence and emotional bonding. The openness of feelings associated with positivism may be reflected in a willingness to risk intimacy coupled with the value of resilience in the event the relationship does not work out.

CHAPTER FOUR

DEAF AMERICANS OF WHITE EUROPEAN DESCENT

Introduction

The Deaf Community is a co-cultural group in the United States that has been long neglected by but is gaining attention from interpersonal communication researchers. "Membership in a deaf community is achieved through (1) identification with the deaf world, (2) shared experiences that come of being hearing-impaired, and (3) participating in the community's activities" (Higgins 1980, 38). The capital "D" in the term "Deaf Culture" is used to purposely differentiate a cultural identification from a physical impairment. "Hearing itself holds little value in identifying membership in the culture... The single unifying bonding force in the culture is the language used, ASL (American Sign Language)" (Norman 1995, 7).

The importance of this unique cultural distinction to the study of interpersonal communication is that communication is the central defining issue. Also, as Cohen (1994) points out, although the Deaf are a cultural group who want to preserve their cultural identity, their culture is usually not conferred by family at birth. Indeed, 70 to 89 percent of Deaf individuals are born to hearing families (Padden and Humphries 1988). For such families,

Parent and child belong to different cultures... And deaf children acquire a sense of cultural identity from their peers rather than their parents, as homosexuals do. But the crucial

49

issue is that hearing parent and deaf child don't share a means of communication. Deaf children cannot grasp their (hearing) parents' spoken language, and hearing parents are unlikely to know sign language. Communication is not a gift automatically bestowed in infancy but an acquisition gained only by laborious effort. (Dolnick 1993, 37–38)

In an ethnographic study of deafness, culture, coping, and stigma, Keane-Dawes (1995) discovered that in the U.S. deaf population she studied, Deaf Culture was a significant part of identity for white individuals of European descent, but not for African American individuals. Keane-Dawes (1995) provides strong evidence that although some African Americans who are deaf may identify with Deaf Culture, it is by no means a central identifying force—as it is for White Americans of European descent who are deaf.

Deaf Culture, if it exists in the community of African American individuals who are deaf, is simply not the same as Deaf Culture as it has been documented among white Americans (see especially Padden and Humphries 1988). Keane-Dawes (1995) argues that the racial climate in the United States makes racial lines so pervasive in determining cultural identity as to overshadow the identity created by participation in the community of the hearing impaired. In addition, she points out that within the interracial deaf community, there are racial exclusions; many of her African American respondents felt unable to identify with Deaf Culture, which they described as reflective of white interests and agendas. To further underscore this point, her white respondents did not recognize the exclusion. They did not recognize that their values and beliefs might not be shared by African Americans who are also deaf. In short, Keane-Dawes concludes that the cultural issues related to racial identity in an interracial (but majority white) deaf community serve to exclude African American individuals from fully identifying with Deaf Culture. Keane-Dawe's (1995) findings warrant the use of caution in generalizing an assumption of American Deaf Cultural identity beyond White Americans of European descent. Because the present study draws upon the same population, it is confined to Deaf Culture of White Americans of European descent.

Research Questions

This chapter provides an investigation that examines Propositions 1 and 3 for White Deaf Americans of European descent. Proposition 1 states that perceived self-concept support is the basis of interpersonal attraction. As stated in Chapter One, two research questions were posed to discover the culturally-specific attributes and levels of mate relationships.

RQ1a: What are the attributes of mate relationships?

RQ1b: What are the levels of mate relationships?

Proposition 3 states that different types of self-concept support are the basis for *entry* into and increasing *intensity* of interpersonal relationships. The following research question was posed to discover the culture-specific nature of the attributes elicited by the pursuit of RQ1a, above.

RQ2: Which attributes are *entry* and which are *intensity* variables?

Procedures

As described in Chapter One, the method for identification of attributes and levels was twofold. First, open-ended surveys were distributed. These surveys asked respondents to list attributes of the mate relationship. Then, respondents were asked to list the levels (stages) through which mate relationships progress from least to most intimate. The results of these questions were used to identify the most commonly mentioned attributes (RQ1a) and levels (RQ1b). In this first stage of data collection, participants were also asked several questions that were used to explore RQs 3, 4, and 5. Analysis of these data are presented in Chapters Seven and Eight.

For the second stage of data collection, the selected labels for attributes and levels were arrayed in a Galileo (see Chapter One) questionnaire in paired comparisons of attributes with levels (RQ2); levels with the concepts "ideal mate," "commitment," and with the most intimate level in the sequence (RQ1b). Several other paired comparisons were included for examination of RQs that are explored in Chapters Seven and Eight. This second survey was distributed to a second sample. Both surveys also included basic questions about demographics and relationship history. The answers to these basic questions were used for sample description.

Samples

The first survey was distributed to twenty-five undergraduate students enrolled in a communication course at a small predominantly white university for the deaf and hearing impaired. In addition to white students of European descent, the respondents included four individuals whose surveys were dropped from this analysis: one Hispanic, one Native American, one mixed race individual, and one international student.

The remaining sample for this study included seventeen males and four females with an average age of twenty-six years. Regarding relational history, thirteen respondents indicated that they were currently involved in a mate-type opposite sex relationship; three respondents were married and one was divorced. All but two remaining participants indicated that they had been involved in mate-type opposite sex relationships in the past. All respondents indicated that they perceive themselves to be members of Deaf Culture.

The second survey was distributed to thirty-five students enrolled in a communication course at the same university. There was no overlap between the two samples. Ten surveys had to be dropped from this analysis (two African Americans, two Hispanics, one Asian American, one Native American, two mixed race individuals, and two international students). The remaining sample consisted of twelve males and thirteen females, with an average age of twenty-three years. No participants had ever been married; one was engaged. All participants indicated that they were either currently or had in the past been involved in mate-type opposite sex relationships. All participants indicated that they considered themselves to be members of Deaf Culture.

Results and Interpretation

Research Question 1a. As described in Chapter One, the first research question, seeking to identify salient attributes of the mate relationship, was answered with responses to the question in the first survey that asked respondents to list at least ten "characteristics of a mate-type (dating, romantic) relationship." Table 4.1 contains these results.

A total of eighty-six attributes were mentioned; sixty of these were mentioned only once and are not included in the table. Of the twenty-six attributes mentioned by more than one respondent, eight were mentioned by at least thirty percent of the sample. These are FUN, COMMUNICATION, HONESTY, LOVE, AFFECTION, SUPPORT, SEXUAL ATTRATION, TRUST, and FRIENDSHIP. These nine attributes were included in the second (Galileo) survey to assess their status as entry or intensity variables. Although all of the three traditionally assumed (see Cushman and Cahn 1985 and Nicotera and Associates 1993) intensity variables (affection, respect, and support) were mentioned, only one (SEXUAL ATTRACTION) of the traditional assumed entry variables (physical attractiveness, sexual appeal, and intelligence) was mentioned. This indicates that cultural generalities from the traditional research cannot be generalized to Deaf Culture. SEXUAL ATTRACTION met the thirty-percent criterion. Although it did not, RESPECT was included in the second survey for its consideration regarding RQ2 (assessment as entry or intensity variable). Because the remaining traditional variables were not mentioned by even one respondent as salient attributes of the mate relationship, they were not included in the second survey.

Research Question 1b. As described in Chapter One, this research question, seeking to identify salient labels for increasing levels of the mate relationship, was answered with responses to the question in the first survey that asked respondents to "list the stages a mate-type (dating, romantic) relationship goes through as it progresses from least to most intimate." These data were subjected to a qualitative analysis. The lists were examined for commonalities and patterns, and a general set of stages was generated. This general set of stages was then compared to each individual list and refined until it was judged that the general list was a fair represen-

Table 4.1 Mateship Attributes for Deaf White Americans
of European Descent

ATTRIBUTES	% MALES	% FEMALES	% TOTAL
fun	0	47	53
communication	50	47	47
honesty	50	47	47
love	50	40	42
affection	25	33	32
support	50	27	32
sexual attraction	75	20	32
trust	0	40	32
friendship	0	40	32
sharing	50	20	26
caring	25	20	21
humor	25	20	21
faithful	25	13	16
kissing	25	13	16
listens	25	13	16
do things together	50	7	16
companionship	0	20	16
talking	0	20	16
warm	0	20	16
creative/original	25	7	11
help each other	25	7	11
motivated	25	7	11
best friend	0	13	11
easy going	0	13	11
patience	0	13	11
respect	0	13	11
touch	0	13	11

tation of all individual lists. As a final caution, a research assistant compared each individual list against the general list to be sure the general list did not contradict any individual list. The general list included the following levels, each subsequent level representing an increase in intimacy: CASUAL DATE, STEADY DATE, ENGAGED, and MARRIAGE.

This list of stages was then subjected to a quantitative analysis using the second (Galileo) survey. The paired comparisons in the Galileo survey included the concepts "ideal mate" and "commitment" paired with each relationship level. The mean values of these distances were used to quantitatively verify the progression of stages generated qualitatively. These results are presented in Table 4.2. The table shows that the mean distances from each indicator of intimacy (ideal mate and commitment) do not progressively decrease as the level designation increases. The sequence of levels does, however, somewhat depict increasing levels of mateship intimacy.

In addition to the analysis of mean distances from ideal mate and commitment, z-scores of difference were computed so that all level designations were compared on their mean distances from the most intimate level (MARRIAGE) and from the concepts COMMITMENT and IDEAL MATE. These results are presented in Tables 4.3 and 4.4.

The labels for mateship levels are, in sequence, CASUAL DATE, STEADY DATE, ENGAGED, and MARRIAGE The z-scores of difference in Table 4.3 represent the differences between the mean distances of

Table 4.2 Mateship Levels for Deaf White Americans of European Decent

	IDEAL MATE	COMMITMENT
CASUAL DATE	78.08	111.56
STEADY DATE	88.67	86.04
ENGAGED	42.76	65.80
MARRIAGE	39.38	69.80

Table 4.3 Z-scores of Difference Between Mateship
Levels on Distances From Most Intimate Level: Deaf
White Americans of European Descent

	CASUAL DATE	STEADY DATE	ENGAGED
STEADY DATE	0.05		
ENGAGED	1.06	0.96	
MARRIED	2.18*	2.02*	2.10*

*p<.05

each level from the top end of the scale (MARRIAGE); for example the
figure .05, between CASUAL DATE and STEADY DATE, represents the z-
score of the difference between the mean distance of CASUAL DATE
with MARRIAGE and the mean distance of STEADY DATE with MAR-
RIAGE. As shown in Table 4.3, STEADY DATE is not significantly closer to marriage than CASUAL DATE, the previous level in the
sequence. The next level, ENGAGED, is not significantly closer to
MARRIAGE than is STEADY DATE. ENGAGED is also not significantly
closer to marriage than is CASUAL DATE. However, all three of these
are significantly different in their mean distance from MARRIAGE
than MARRIAGE is in its distance from itself (zero). The first three
levels are not significantly different from one another in terms of
their distance from MARRIAGE. These results show only two functional levels—DATING (general) and MARRIAGE.

The statistical significance of the levels as different designations of increasing levels of mateship was further investigated by
examining the differences between the levels regarding their mean
distances from COMMITMENT and IDEAL MATE. Table 4.4 presents
these results. Table 4.4 shows that CASUAL DATE, STEADY DATE, and
ENGAGED do not represent a significant progression of concepts in
relation to either COMMITMENT or IDEAL MATE. In fact, the only significant difference is that between CASUAL DATE and MARRIAGE in
their degree of COMMITMENT. The sequence generated qualitatively

Table 4.4 Z-scores of Difference Between Mateship
Levels on Distances From Commitment and Ideal Mate:
Deaf White Americans of European Descent

	CASUAL DATE	STEADY DATE	ENGAGED	MARRIAGE
CASUAL DATE		0.87	1.48	1.17
STEADY DATE	0.24		1.55	0.48
ENGAGED	1.89	0.58		0.11
MARRIAGE	2.03*	1.17	0.29	

upper half=COMMITMENT
lower half=IDEAL MATE
*p<.05

does not represent a statistically significant progression of stages
toward mateship commitment. This may be due to language difficulties. These students use English as a second language, their
native language being ASL. This issue is addressed below.

Research Question 2. As explained in Chapter One, this RQ asks
which mateship variables operate as entry variables and which as
intensity variables. To adequately test this RQ, the mean distances between the attributes (identified in analysis for RQ1a—
FUN, COMMUNICATION, HONESTY, LOVE, AFFECTION, SUPPORT, SEXUAL
ATTRACTION, TRUST, FRIENDSHIP, and RESPECT) need to be examined
in light of their relationships with mateship stages. Because the
data did not reveal a stable and significant progression of stages
for commitment and ideal mateness, this RQ cannot be fully
explored. However, since CASUAL DATE and MARRIAGE were shown to
be significantly different from each other and in their distances
from IDEAL MATE, these two levels can be used as an exploratory
investigation of RQ2.

Recall that entry variables are those attributes whose mean distances to the levels remain stable across levels; intensity variables are those whose mean distances become progressively smaller as the levels increase in intimacy. These progressions can be statistically verified by the computation of z-scores of difference, which reveal whether progressive relationship levels are significantly different in their respective mean distances from the attributes in question.

Table 4.5 Mean Distances Between
Attributes and Levels: Deaf White
Americans of European Descent

	CASUAL DATE	MARRIAGE
fun	67.4	284.17
communication	57.4	69.64
honesty	76	66.75
love	74.4	55.71
affection	78.2	48.63
support	78.33	46.54
sexual attraction	106.52	72.08
trust	102	61.88
friendship	111.80	164.17
respect	68.8	25.21

Table 4.5 shows that not all the attributes are progressively closer to the more intimate mateship level, indicating that these variables may not be important characteristics of the mate relationship. The more important analysis, however, appears in Table 4.6, which shows whether these differences between distances from the two mateship levels are significant. The z-scores in Table 4.6 indicate that only one attribute, RESPECT, is significantly closer to MARRIAGE than to CASUAL DATE. In this exploratory analysis, RESPECT may be an intensity variable; whereas the other attributes may be entry variables. Because of the inability to generate a significant set of stages, these results cannot be considered conclusive.

Table 4.6 Z-scores of Difference
Between Subsequent Levels On
Distances From Attributes: Deaf
White Americans of European
Descent

	CASUAL DATE AND MARRIAGE
fun	1.02
communication	0.39
honesty	0.19
love	0.55
affection	1.15
support	1.32
sexual attraction	1.01
trust	1.02
friendship	0.89
respect	2.99*

Conclusions

Before considering any of the results for attributes and levels specifically, it is necessary to discuss the issue of conducting such surveys in a language other than the respondents' native language. All of the participants in this study are native users of ASL; English is their second language. During the administration of the surveys, the respondents requested a great deal of explanation. Although they seemed more comfortable with the first survey, which was open-ended and more straightforward, they required a great deal of explanation and asked for numerous examples before they were able to attend to the task. Even with this first survey, the respondents did not seem as comfortable with the question about relationship stages. The concept of stages or phases in relationships was particularly difficult to interpret from English to ASL.

Because I am not fluent in ASL, the students' own instructor acted as interpreter. As it became clear that a language interpretation of my explanation was not sufficient, the instructor stepped in with explanations she knew as well-suited to the learning needs and styles both generally of native users of ASL and of these students in particular. The crucial element of explanation was to give copious examples. This may be a better explanation than any other for the normative set of mateship stages that emerged from the data.

In attempting to make sense of the results from the second survey, I again consulted with the instructor. She was not confident that the students came to an understanding of the instructions. She assessed that in most cases the Galileo survey was probably completed in the spirit of cooperation with little understanding of what was requested on the survey. Very little confidence is placed in these results. The results of the Galileo survey analysis should be considered inconclusive, and should be used only to generate questions for further research in this population.

The failure to obtain conclusive results with this survey method is an important lesson in dealing with Deaf populations. This population (Deaf Culture) may not respond to written language in the same way that native users (speakers and lip-readers) of spoken English do. Because their non-written language is ASL, their cultural use of written English is probably quite different than that of populations who both converse and write in English. The dynamics of meaning for a population who converse and write in two different languages is undoubtedly complex and unique. This is an important consideration for communication researchers investigating Deaf populations. In her study using focus groups, Keane-Dawes (1995) obtained rich, thoughtful, and insightful responses. It seems that such face-to-face interviewing techniques are better suited than surveys of any kind for obtaining data that give insight into this cultural group.

Even so, data that can be confidently assessed is the list of attributes, the open-ended data on quality (Chapter Eight), and the open-ended data on conflict sources (Chapter Seven). The list of attributes generated by the open-ended survey is consistent with the literature on mate relationships. For Deaf Americans of European descent, a mate relationship is characterized by fun, communication, honesty, love, affection, support, sexual attraction, trust, friendship, and respect. The fact that FUN leads the list is an important piece of cultural information. Simple enjoyment in the context of the relationship was the most frequently mentioned attribute. Unlike the other American cultural groups, intelligence and physical attractiveness were not at all salient. As has been shown in previous chapters, the lack of support for the traditional variables is an important indicator of the dangers of assuming generalizations across U.S. populations, across co-cultures, and across time.

It is quite likely that the mateship levels generated in this study are due more to explanatory examples given during the administration of the open-ended survey than a real reflection of the culture. Because only the first and last levels were used in the analysis of attributes, however, we might generate some questions for future research. Respect is the only intensity variable identified; the question of whether respect is indeed an intensity variable is interesting. Recall that respect was found to operate as an entry variable for the hearing population of White Americans of European descent and an intensity variable for African Americans. It may be that the increase in respect required for relationship growth is related to cultural identification with a traditionally marginalized group. Of course, this is pure speculation, as the results of the present study are inconclusive. Future research comparing Deaf cultural (European American) norms for mate relationships with norms for hearing European American culture seems warranted.

CHAPTER FIVE

REPRESENTING CARRIBEAN CULTURE: JAMAICA

Introduction

As explained in Chapter One, Jamaican culture was included for two reasons. First, almost no research on human communication processes has been conducted with this cultural group. Second, Jamaican culture is a unique blend—with African, British, European, North American, Central American, South American, and Asian influences. Jamaican culture can be described as high-context (Keane-Dawes 1995). Due to colonialism and the distribution of wealth in Jamaica, there are important stratifications in the culture: capitalists (owners of the means of production); larger farmers; upper middle class and intelligentsia; small farmers and peasants; lower middle class; and the working class (Keane-Dawes 1995; Manley 1990). This last is the largest; the typical Jamaican is a member of the working class. "A communal instinct lurks in the consciousness of the average (Jamaican). This Jamaican displays to a remarkable degree an instinct for 'good works'" (Manley 1990, 48). Keane-Dawes (1995), a Jamaican herself, speculates that this instinct for "good works" is part of a cultural ideology that also values the maintenance of good personal relationships. Until now, no communication study of personal relationships has been conducted in this culture. This research represents an important step in the application of communication theory to Jamaican culture.

Research Questions

This chapter provides an investigation that examines Propositions 1 and 3 for Jamaicans. Proposition 1 states that perceived self-concept support is the basis of interpersonal attraction. As stated in Chapter One, two research questions were posed to discover the culturally-specific attributes and levels of mate relationships.

RQ1a: What are the attributes of mate relationships?

RQ1b: What are the levels of mate relationships?

Proposition 3 states that different types of self-concept support are the basis for *entry* into and increasing *intensity* of interpersonal relationships. The following research question was posed to discover the culture-specific nature of the attributes elicited by the pursuit of RQ1a, above.

RQ2:   Which attributes are entry and which are intensity variables?

Procedures

As described in Chapter One, the method for identification of attributes and levels was twofold. First, open-ended surveys were distributed. These surveys asked respondents to list attributes of the mate relationship. Then, respondents were asked to list the levels (stages) through which mate relationships progress from least to most intimate. The results of these questions were used to identify the most commonly mentioned attributes (RQ1a) and levels (RQ1b). In this first stage of data collection, participants were also asked several questions that were used to explore RQs 3, 4, and 5. Analyses of these data are presented in Chapters Seven and Eight.

For the second stage of data collection, the selected labels for attributes and levels were arrayed in a Galileo (see Chapter One) questionnaire in paired comparisons of attributes with levels (RQ2); levels with the concepts "ideal mate," "commitment," and with the most intimate level in the sequence (RQ1b). Several other paired comparisons were included for examination of RQs that are explored in Chapters Seven and Eight. This second survey was distributed to a second sample. Both surveys also included basic questions about demographics and relationship history. The answers to these basic questions were used for sample description.

Samples

The first survey was distributed to twenty-three undergraduate students enrolled in communication courses at two Jamaican colleges. In addition to twenty-two students of African descent, the respondents included one individual of European descent whose survey was dropped from this analysis. The remaining sample for this study included ten males and twelve females with an average age of twenty years. Regarding relational history, sixteen respondents indicated that they were currently involved in a mate-type opposite sex relationship; none were married, engaged, or cohabiting. All remaining participants indicated that they had been involved in mate-type opposite sex relationships in the past.

The second survey was distributed to seventy-one students enrolled in communication courses at the same colleges. There was no overlap between the two samples. Twelve surveys had to be dropped from this analysis (four Indians, two Trinidadians, two Barbadians, and four mixed race individuals). The remaining sample consisted of sixteen males and forty-three females, with an average age of twenty-one years. The majority of the sample (fifty-five) were single; four were married. All participants indicated that they were either currently or had in the past been involved in mate-type opposite sex relationships.

Results and Interpretation

Research Question 1a. As described in Chapter One, the first research question, seeking to identify salient attributes of the mate relationship, was answered with responses to the question in the first survey that asked respondents to list at least ten "characteristics of a mate-type (dating, romantic) relationship." Table 5.1 contains these results.

Table 5.1 Mateship Attributes for Jamacians of African Descent

ATTRIBUTES	% MALES	% FEMALES	% TOTAL
trust	60	75	68
love	70	67	68
honesty	40	58	50
respect	20	58	41
communication	30	50	41
understanding	30	50	41
caring	50	33	41
friendship	30	42	36
affection	20	42	32
sharing	20	42	32
compatibility	10	33	23
giving	30	17	23
sex	30	17	23
compromise	0	33	18
faithfulness	0	33	18
considerate	10	25	18
humor	10	25	18
romantic	30	8	18
open	10	17	14
patience	10	17	14
devotion	20	8	14
exciting	20	8	14
sacrificing	20	8	14
adventurous	0	17	9
fun	0	17	9
integrity	0	17	9
sincerity	0	17	9

(Table 5.1 cont.)

ATTRIBUTES	% MALES	% FEMALES	% TOTAL
kind	10	8	9
mature	10	8	9
physically attractive	10	8	9
support	10	8	9
commitment	20	0	9
spontaneous	20	0	9
intelligence	0	8	5
sex appeal	10	0	5

A total of sixty-nine attributes were mentioned; thirty-seven of these were mentioned only once and are not included in the table (except for INTELLIGENCE and SEXUALLY APPEALING, explained below). Of the thirty-two attributes mentioned by more than one respondent, ten were mentioned by at least thirty percent of the sample. These are TRUST, LOVE, HONESTY, RESPECT, COMMUNICATION, UNDERSTANDING, CARING, FRIENDSHIP, AFFECTION, and SHARING. These ten attributes were included in the second (Galileo) survey to assess their status as entry or intensity variables. Two of the traditionally assumed U.S. intensity variables (RESPECT and AFFECTION) are on this list. The third (SUPPORT) was mentioned by two individuals. The three traditionally assumed U.S. entry variables were also mentioned; PHYSICALLY ATTRACTIVE by two individuals, INTELLIGENCE and SEXUALLY APPEALING each by one individual. To compare patterns surrounding these attributes between Jamaicans of African descent and Americans of African descent, the four traditional attributes that did not meet the thirty percent criterion were included in the second survey for their consideration regarding RQ2 (assessment as entry or intensity variables): SUPPORT, PHYSICALLY ATTRACTIVE, INTELLIGENCE, and SEXUALLY APPEALING. All attributes considered in RQ2 are printed in boldface in Table 5.1.

Research Question 1b. As described in Chapter One, this research question, seeking to identify salient labels for increasing levels of the mate relationship, was answered with responses to the question in the first survey that asked respondents to "list the stages a mate-type (dating, romantic) relationship goes through as it progresses from least to most intimate." These data were subjected to a qualitative analysis. The lists were examined for commonalities and patterns, and a general set of stages was generated. This general set of stages was then compared to each individual list and refined until it was judged that the general list was a fair representation of all individual lists. As a final caution, a research assistant compared each individual list against the general list to be sure the general list did not contradict any individual list. The general list included the following levels, each subsequent level representing an increase in intimacy: DATING, LOVERS, LONG-TERM COUPLE, and MARRIAGE.

This list of stages was then subjected to a quantitative analysis using the second (Galileo) survey. The paired comparisons in the Galileo survey included the concepts "ideal mate" and "commitment" (as for the two hearing American samples, the latter coincidentally also appeared on the list of attributes, but did not meet the thirty percent criterion) paired with each relationship level. The mean values of these distances were used to quantitatively verify the progression of stages generated qualitatively. These results are presented in Table 5.2. The table shows that the mean distances from each indicator of intimacy (ideal mate and commitment) do indeed decrease as the level designation increases. The sequence of levels does depict increasing levels of mateship intimacy.

In addition to the analysis of mean distances from ideal mate and commitment, z-scores of difference were computed so that all

Table 5.2   Mateship Levels for Jamacians of African Descent

	IDEAL MATE	COMMITMENT
DATING	74.15	87.57
LOVER	50.87	31.43
LONG-TERM COUPLE	49.87	22.73
MARRIAGE	31.88	11.02

Table 5.3 Z-scores of Difference Between Mateship Levels on
Distances From Most Intimate Level: Jamacians of African Descent

	DATING	LOVER	LONG-TERM COUPLE
DATING			
LOVER	1.72		
LONG-TERM COUPLE	2.06*	1.20	
MARRIAGE	2.77*	4.77*	4.25*

*p<.05

level designations were compared on their mean distances from the
most intimate level (MARRIAGE) and from the concepts COMMITMENT
and IDEAL MATE. These results are presented in Tables 5.3 and 5.4.

The labels for mateship levels are, in sequence, DATING, LOVERS,
LONG-TERM COUPLE, and MARRIAGE. The z-scores of difference in
Table 5.3 represent the differences between the mean distances of
each level from the top end of the scale (MARRIAGE); for example the
figure 1.72, between DATING and LOVER, represents the z-score of
the difference between the mean distance of DATING and MARRIAGE
and the mean distance of LOVER and MARRIAGE. As shown in Table
5.3, LOVER is not significantly closer to MARRIAGE than is DATING, the
previous level in the sequence. However, the next level, LONG-TERM
COUPLE, is significantly closer to MARRIAGE than is DATING. Because
LONG-TERM COUPLE is not significantly closer to MARRIAGE than is
LOVER, LOVER was dropped from the sequence for subsequent analysis. The last step in the sequence, from LONG-TERM COUPLE to MAR-
RIAGE, is significant. Although the sequence of labels does represent increasing levels of ideal mateness and commitment, as shown
in Table 5.2, not every step in the sequence is a statistically significant different degree of mateness.

The statistical significance of the levels as different designations of increasing levels of mateship was further investigated by
examining the differences between the levels regarding their mean

Table 5.4 Z-scores of Difference Between Mateship Levels on Distances From Commitment and Ideal Mate: Jamacians of African Descent

	DATING	LOVER	LONG-TERM COUPLE	MARRIAGE
DATING		2.13*	2.44*	2.85*
LOVER	0.81		1.07	2.24*
LONG-TERM COUPLE	0.83	0.04		1.23
MARRIAGE	1.85	0.96	0.89	

upper half=COMMITMENT
lower half=IDEAL MATE
*p<.05

distances from COMMITMENT and IDEAL MATE. Table 5.4 presents these results. Table 5.4 shows that none of the steps in the sequence represent a significant increase in ideal mateness. However, significantly increasing degrees of commitment can be seen. LOVER represents a significantly greater degree of commitment than DATING. LONG-TERM COUPLE and LOVER are not significantly different concepts in relation to COMMITMENT, nor are MARRIAGE and LONG-TERM COUPLE. However, MARRIAGE is significantly closer to COMMITMENT than both LOVER and DATING.

The decision to drop LOVER from the sequence was substantiated. It was difficult to determine what final set of stages to use for further analysis because LONG-TERM COUPLE and MARRIAGE are not significantly different degrees of commitment. In fact, although permanent commitments or future plans for such permanence were frequently mentioned, the term "marriage" was explicitly mentioned by only fourteen percent of the first sample. Anecdotal knowledge of Jamaican culture suggests that the institutionalization of a personal relationship is not seen as an indicator of the state of the relationship itself. "Long-term couple" or an equivalent phrase was used as a stage designation by thirty-eight percent of the first sample. It was decided to examine two alternative two-step sequences, DATING to LONG-TERM COUPLE and DATING to MARRIAGE. Each step in these sequences represents a significant increase in the degree of commitment, which is a concrete operationalization of the more abstract term "ideal mate" (see Chapter One). Since LONG-TERM COUPLE and MARRIAGE are not significantly different levels of mateship, this step is not examined further.

Research Question 2. As explained in Chapter One, this RQ asks which mateship variables operate as entry variables and which as intensity variables. The mean distances between the attributes (identified in analysis for RQ1a—TRUST, LOVE HONESTY, RESPECT, COMMUNICATION, UNDERSTANDING, CARING, FRIENDSHIP, AFFECTION, SHARING, PHYSICALLY ATTRACTIVE, SUPPORT, INTELLIGENCE, and SEX APPEAL) and the significant mateship levels were examined. Entry variables are those attributes whose mean distances to the levels remain stable across levels; intensity variables are those whose mean distances become progressively smaller as the levels increase in intimacy. These progressions were statistically verified by the computation of z-scores of difference which reveal whether progressive relationship levels are significantly different in their respective mean distances from the attributes in question.

Table 5.5 shows that all the attributes are progressively closer to more intimate mateship levels, indicating that each is an important characteristic of the mate relationship. The more important analysis, however, appears in Table 5.6, which shows whether these mean distances become significantly closer to higher mateship levels. Those that do not can be labeled entry variables; those that do can be labeled intensity variables. The z-scores in Table 5.6 reveal identical results for the sequence DATING to LONG-TERM COUPLE and the sequence DATING to MARRIAGE. Two attributes are not significantly closer to either LONG-TERM COUPLE or to MARRIAGE than to DATING. Hence, these attributes operate as entry variables: PHYSICAL ATTRACTIVENESS and INTELLIGENCE. The remaining attributes are significantly closer to more intimate mateship levels. Hence, these attributes operate as intensity variables: TRUST, LOVE, HONESTY, RESPECT, COMMUNICATION, UNDERSTANDING, CARING, FRIENDSHIP, AFFECTION, SHARING, SUPPORT, and SEX APPEAL.

Table 5.5   Mean Distances Between Attributes and Levels: Jamacians of African Descent

ATTRIBUTE	DATING	LONG-TERM COUPLE	MARRIAGE
trust	51.15	16.19	7.47
love	48.98	11.41	7.02
honesty	48.57	14.38	6.77
respect	33.81	15.00	6.33
communication	41.37	15.27	11.48
understanding	55.22	20.29	8.37
caring	46.44	15.67	8.41
friendship	41.20	24.11	19.29
affection	44.37	18.12	10.55
sharing	44.47	14.59	10.75
physically attractive	37.07	28.42	24.07
support	50.25	18.74	10.78
intelligence	259.43	73.11	48.36
sex appeal	71.10	14.68	9.16

Conclusions

As with the other cultures examined thus far, the list of attributes generated by the open-ended survey is consistent with the literature on mate relationships. For Jamaicans of African descent, a mate relationship is characterized by trust, love, honesty, respect, communication, understanding, caring, friendship, affection, and sharing. Although of lesser salience to the sample in this study, the relationship is also characterized by perceptions of physical attraction, support, intelligence, and sex appeal. As a whole, this list of fourteen attributes includes the six "traditional" crucial attributes for "U.S. culture" (see Nicotera and Associates 1993). The fact that four of these attributes did not pass the thirty percent criterion is an important indicator, once again, that these attributes

Table 5.6 Z-scores of Difference Between Subsequent Levels on
Distances From Attributes: Jamaicans of African Descent

	DATING and L-T COUPLE	DATING and MARRIAGE
trust	6.54*	9.39*
love	7.11*	8.06*
honesty	6.30*	8.41*
respect	3.76*	5.96*
communication	2.75*	3.17*
understanding	3.11*	4.34*
caring	5.31*	6.78*
friendship	2.74*	3.54*
affection	4.49*	5.93*
sharing	5.63*	6.44*
physically attractive	1.08	1.56
support	5.31*	6.59*
intelligence	1.02	1.16
sex appeal	2.48*	2.73*

$*p<.05$

may not be as crucial as has been assumed. It also illustrates once
again the dangers of assuming generalizations across cultures.
However, at the same time, the fact that all six did appear confirms
the validity of past research. The power of these fourteen attributes
in addressing relational maintenance and quality are addressed in
Chapters Seven and Eight.

The mateship levels that were identified in this study are similar in character but different in semantic content from the other
cultures examined and from past research in this tradition.
Qualitatively, the mate relationship progresses through the following stages: dating, lover, long-term couple, and marriage, each
level representing a quantitatively greater degree of commitment

and ideal mateness. Statistical analysis showed, however, that these stages are somewhat redundant. By analyzing significant differences between subsequent stages, the list was reduced to two alternative two-stage sequences: dating to long-term couple and dating to marriage. In comparison to the other cultures examined and to past research, these sets of stages are developmentally similar to the sequences found for other cultures as well as to the sequence which has traditionally been accepted in this line of work.

There are two important functional differences between the traditional labels (casual date, steady date, fiancee, and spouse) and the labels found in this study. First, the statistically significant levels in this study do not differentiate casual from serious or steady dating—although the nonsignificant step from dating to lover may be seen as such a qualitative differentiation. Second, these data do not specify a stage that is a precursor to marriage (or permanence). In fact, the concept of "engagement" was not mentioned in any form by the respondents to the open-ended survey, even by those few who mentioned "marriage."

The nature of the attributes as entry or intensity variables is another area that only partially supports the past research in this tradition. Of the three traditionally accepted entry variables (physical attractiveness, sexual attraction, and intelligence), two were found to operate as an entry variables in Jamaican culture: physical attractiveness and intelligence. Self-concept support of the other on physical attractiveness and intelligence need not increase for the relationship to develop. Sex appeal operates as an intensity variable in Jamaican culture. The study shows that self-concept support of the other on sex appeal does need to increase for the relationship to progress. In fact, sexual matters seem to be of paramount importance in discussing the mate relationship in this culture. Several respondents added comments to the surveys that suggest that sexual activity is a crucial part of the development of the mate relationship.

The traditionally accepted intensity variables are respect, support, and affection. Jamaican culture follows this pattern. Progression to deeper stages of intimacy requires that these variables increase. All the additional variables revealed in this study operate as intensity variables. Trust, love, honesty, communication, understanding, caring, friendship, and sharing must continually increase for the pair to progress to deeper intimacy and commitment.

All but one of the attributes (sharing) discovered for Jamaican culture are also salient for either European American culture or for African American culture (or for both). In Jamaican culture, the following attributes operate identically to both European and African American cultures: trust, honesty, caring, affection, physical attraction, and support. Several attributes operate identically in Jamaican and African American cultures: respect, communication, understanding, and intelligence. Sex appeal, however, operates differently in Jamaican culture than in either U.S. co-culture. These and other cultural comparisons, in addition to comparisons with Deaf European American culture, will be considered further in Chapter Nine.

Although this study has revealed somewhat different results from the U.S. co-cultures examined and from past research in this tradition, the general theoretic structure is supported. In addition, the general methodology has been once again shown to be fruitful. The importance of applying communication theory to Jamaican culture is highlighted. The development and maintenance of personal relationships are primary values for Jamaicans (Keane-Dawes, 1995); yet few communication researchers have ventured into this cultural environment to examine these phenomena.

CHAPTER SIX

JAPAN

Yanan Ju (in Nicotera and Associates 1993) asserts that "mate selection theorists have predominantly been Western-biased, their work heavily laden with Western values; they have generated theories and models with a discernable imprint of 'free choice.' Their studies, therefore, may have reduced significance for more traditional, non-Western cultures" (201). It is important to continue the work of testing and extending Cushman's rules theory of interpersonal relationship development (Cushman and Cahn 1985; Cushman, Valentinsen, and Dietrich 1982; Nicotera and Associates 1993) in non-Western cultures.

As explained in Chapter One, Japanese culture is included in this research because only one study has been conducted in this research tradition (Ju, in Nicotera and Associates 1993), which stopped at identifying crucial attributes of the mate relationship. None of the propositions has been tested in Japanese culture. Ju's study (in Nicotera and Associates 1993) identified a rank ordering of importance for eleven crucial mateship attributes; however, the attributes were supplied to the respondents. Ju's mateship attributes study was part of a larger study of cultural change of Japan, China, and Korea. Given this larger focus, the attributes were drawn from knowledge of East Asian cultural traditions surrounding mate selection, gained from consultation with prominent scholars and based on a pretest.

The goal of comparison among the three cultures (Japan, China, and Korea) necessitated the identical lists. Respondents were asked to select from the list the three most important factors in selecting a marriage partner. The attributes were then rank ordered according to the percentage of the sample that selected each attribute as one of their three choices. In Ju's study, Japanese respondents ranked mateship attributes as follows: Love (64.4 percent), Emotional Compatibility (53.8 percent); High Moral Standards (46.0 percent); Work Ability (35.4 percent); Occupation (22.6 percent); Family Financial Condition (21.5 percent); Common Interest (21.1 percent); Age (6.8 percent); Education (6.4 percent); Looks (4.3 percent); and Family Social Position (2.7 percent).

This chapter expands on Ju's beginning by identifying attributes from open-ended questions to assess those that are most salient for Japanese culture. This study continues the pursuit of testing in Asian culture the propositions posited in Nicotera and Associates (1993) and summarized in Chapter One.

Research Questions

This chapter provides an investigation that examines Propositions 1 and 3 for Japanese students. Proposition 1 states that perceived self-concept support is the basis of interpersonal attraction. As stated in Chapter One, two research questions were posed to discover the culturally-specific attributes and levels of mate relationships.

RQ1a: What are the attributes of mate relationships?

RQ1b: What are the levels of mate relationships?

Proposition 3 states that different types of self-concept support are the basis for *entry* into and increasing *intensity* of interpersonal relationships. The following research question was posed to discover the culture-specific nature of the attributes elicited by the pursuit of RQ1a, above.

RQ2:   Which attributes are entry and which are intensity variables?

Procedures

As described in Chapter One, the method for identification of attributes and levels was twofold. First, open-ended surveys were distributed. These surveys asked respondents to list attributes of the mate relationship. Then, respondents were asked to list the levels (stages) through which mate relationships progress from least to most intimate. The results of these questions were used to identify the most commonly mentioned attributes (RQ1a) and levels (RQ1b). This survey was followed by a discussion among a facilitator and the respondents. Although there is overlap between the females' and males' lists of attributes, it was clear from the discussion that male and female understandings of the mate relationship were quite distinct. It was decided that data from male and female respondents would be analyzed separately, with a general analysis provided where the concepts of the two samples overlapped.

For the second stage of data collection, the selected labels for attributes and levels were arrayed in a Galileo (see Chapter One) questionnaire in paired comparisons of attributes with levels (RQ2); levels with the concepts "ideal mate," "self," and with each other (RQ1b). This second survey was distributed to a second sample. Both surveys also included basic questions about demographics.

Samples

The first survey was distributed to forty undergraduate students enrolled at a large Japanese university. The sample included twenty males and twenty females with an average age of nineteen years. The second survey was distributed to eighty-two students enrolled at the same university. There was no overlap between the two samples. The sample consisted of thirty-two males and thirty-two females, with an average age of nineteen years.

Results and Interpretation

Research Question 1a. As described in Chapter One, the first research question, seeking to identify salient attributes of the mate relationship, was answered with responses to the question in the first survey that asked respondents to list "characteristics of a mate-type (dating, romantic) relationship." Table 6.1 contains these results.

Table 6.1 Japanese Mateship Attributes

ATTRIBUTES: MALES	%	ATTRIBUTES: FEMALES	%
beautiful	65	**love**	85
good cook	50	**wealthy**	75
kind	45	**fun**	70
youth	40	**honest**	45
love	40	**sportsman**	40
honest	35	**employed**	35
fun	25	**kind**	30
wealth	20	**happy**	30
good character	20	age	25
cute	20	handsome	15
charming	20	family	15
family	15	active	15
clever	10	tall	10
education	10	intelligence	10
homeowner	10	have many friends	10
race/Japanese	10	humor	10
smaller than me	10	education	5
employed	5	race/Japanese	5
likes motorcycles	5		
only housewife after marriage	5		
sexy	5		
strong	5		

ATTRIBUTES ON BOTH LISTS	%		%
love	63	age reference (youth/age)	33
wealthy	48	employed	20
fun	48	family	15
appearance (beauty/hands)	40	size reference (small/tall)	10
honest	40	education	8
kind	38	race/Japanese	8

A total of twenty-two attributes were mentioned by males, eighteen by females; twelve of these were on both lists (see Table 6.1). For males, six were mentioned by at least thirty percent. These are BEAUTIFUL, GOOD COOK, KIND, YOUTH, LOVE, and HONEST. For females, eight were mentioned by at least thirty percent. These are LOVE, WEALTHY, HONEST, SPORTSMAN, EMPLOYED, KIND, FUN, and HAPPY. Three attributes made the thirty percent criterion for both males and females (KIND, LOVE, and HONEST). All these attributes were included in the second (Galileo) survey to assess their status as entry or intensity variables; separate surveys were prepared for males and females. All attributes considered in RQ2 are printed in boldface in Table 6.1.

Research Question 1b. As described in Chapter One, this research question, seeking to identify salient labels for increasing levels of the mate relationship, was answered with responses to the question in the first survey that asked respondents to "list the stages a mate-type (dating, romantic) relationship goes through as it progresses from least to most intimate." These data were subjected to the same type of qualitative analysis described in previous chapters. The male and female lists were so similar that they were combined to generate a single sequence of stages. However, all quantitative analyses of the list are conducted separately. The general list included the following levels, each subsequent level representing an increase in intimacy: SOMEONE YOU JUST MET, SOMEONE YOU WOULD DATE, BOYFRIEND/GIRLFRIEND, and SOMEONE YOU WOULD BE ENGAGED TO (awkward wording is due to back-translation).

This list of stages was then subjected to quantitative analyses using the second (Galileo) survey. The paired comparisons in the Galileo survey included the concepts "ideal mate" and "self" paired with each relationship level. The mean values of these distances were used to quantitatively verify the progression of stages generated qualitatively. These results are presented in Table 6.2. The table shows that the mean distances from each indicator of intimacy (ideal mate and self) do indeed decrease as the level designation increases up to the last transition point from BOY/GIRLFRIEND to SOMEONE YOU WOULD BE ENGAGED TO. Up to that point, the sequence of levels does depict increasing levels of mateship intimacy as measured by degree of ideal mateness and closeness to the self.

Table 6.2 Mean Distances Between Mateship Levels, Ideal Mate, and Self for Japanese Sample

MALE SAMPLE	IDEAL MATE	SELF
...JUST MET	78.28	80.00
...WOULD DATE	39.35	45.48
GIRLFRIEND	32.33	42.58
...ENGAGED TO	32.90	44.84
FEMALE SAMPLE		
...JUST MET	79.98	75.78
...WOULD DATE	40.87	57.39
BOYFRIEND	33.94	47.98
...ENGAGED TO	34.79	41.56
COMBINED SAMPLE		
...JUST MET	79.34	77.43
...WOULD DATE	40.26	52.60
BOY/GIRLFRIEND	33.31	45.68
...ENGAGED TO	34.04	42.89

In addition to the analysis of mean distances from ideal mate and self, z-scores of difference were computed so that all level designations were compared on their mean distances from the most intimate level (SOMEONE YOU WOULD BE ENGAGED TO), and of each level from each other level. These results are presented in Tables 6.3 and 6.4.

The labels for mateship levels are, in sequence, SOMEONE YOU JUST MET, SOMEONE YOU WOULD DATE, BOY/GIRLFRIEND, and SOMEONE YOU WOULD BE ENGAGED TO. The z-scores of difference in Table 6.3 represent the differences between the mean distances of each level from the top end of the scale (ENGAGED TO); for example the figure 2.31, between JUST MET and WOULD DATE, represents the Z-score of the difference between the mean distance of JUST MET from

Table 6.3 Z-scores of the Difference for Mateship Levels Between
Distances from Most Intimate Level: Japanese Sample

MALE SAMPLE	JUST MET	WOULD DATE	GIRLFRIEND
...JUST MET			
...WOULD DATE	2.31*		
GIRLFRIEND	2.71*	0.34	
...ENGAGED TO	15.26*	8.86*	8.49*
FEMALE SAMPLE	JUST MET	WOULD DATE	BOYFRIEND
...JUST MET			
...WOULD DATE	5.25*		
BOYFRIEND	6.58*	2.10*	
...ENGAGED TO	64.22*	16.98*	10.13*
COMBINED SAMPLE	JUST MET	WOULD DATE	BOY/GIRLFRIEND
...JUST MET			
...WOULD DATE	5.36*		
BOY/GIRLFRIEND	6.97*	1.87	
...ENGAGED TO	41.84*	18.98*	13.89*

*p<.05

Table 6.4 Z-scores of the Difference Between Levels in their Distance From Each Other: Japanese Sample

MALE SAMPLE	JUST MET	WOULD DATE	GIRLFRIEND
...JUST MET			
...WOULD DATE	22.40*		
GIRLFRIEND	22.54*	5.86*	
...ENGAGED TO	15.26*	8.86*	8.49*
FEMALE SAMPLE	**JUST MET**	**WOULD DATE**	**BOYFRIEND**
...JUST MET			
...WOULD DATE	34.32*		
BOYFRIEND	75.91*	7.91*	
...ENGAGED TO	64.22*	16.98*	10.13*
COMBINED SAMPLE	**JUST MET**	**WOULD DATE**	**BOY/GIRLFRIEND**
...JUST MET			
...WOULD DATE	41.95*		
BOY/GIRLFRIEND	57.57*	10.40*	
...ENGAGED TO	41.84*	18.98*	13.89*

*$p < .05$

ENGAGED TO and the mean distance of WOULD DATE from ENGAGED TO for the male sample. As shown in Table 6.3 for the male sample, WOULD DATE is significantly closer to ENGAGED TO than JUST MET, the previous level in the sequence. However, the next level, GIRLFRIEND is not significantly closer to ENGAGED TO than is WOULD DATE. However, ENGAGED TO is significantly closer to itself (zero) than GIRLFRIEND is to ENGAGED TO. For the male sample, the middle two levels are not significantly different in regard to their distances from the most intimate level. For the female sample, and males and females combined, Table 6.3 shows that all four levels are significantly different in regard to their distances from the most intimate level.

Table 6.4 shows the z-scores of the difference between each level in its distance from each other level. For example, in Table 6.4, the figure 22.40 is the z-score of the difference between the distance from JUST MET to JUST MET (zero) and the distance from JUST MET to WOULD DATE. The table shows that all four levels are significantly different for both males and females.

Research Question 2. As explained in Chapter One, this RQ asks which mateship variables operate as entry variables and which as intensity variables. The mean distances between the attributes (identified in analysis for RQ1a—Males: BEAUTIFUL, GOOD COOK, KIND, YOUTH, LOVE, and HONEST; Females: LOVE, WEALTHY, FUN, HONEST, SPORTSMAN, EMPLOYED, KIND, and HAPPY; Both: KIND, LOVE, and HONEST) and the levels SOMEONE YOU JUST MET, SOMEONE YOU WOULD DATE, BOY/GIRLFRIEND, SOMEONE YOU WOULD BE ENGAGED TO were examined. Entry variables are those attributes whose mean distances to the levels remain stable across levels; intensity variables are those whose mean distances become progressively smaller as the levels increase in intimacy. These progressions were statistically verified by the computation of Z-scores of difference that reveal whether progressive relationship levels are significantly different in their respective mean distances from the attributes in question.

Before drawing conclusions about the results in Tables 6.5 and 6.6, it is important to consider the nature of the transition between the mateship levels. The transition between SOMEONE YOU JUST MET and SOMEONE YOU WOULD DATE is the juncture at which the pair actually enters a mate-type relationship. Any significant difference

Table 6.5 Mean Distances Between Attributes and Levels:
Japanese Sample

MALE SAMPLE	JUST MET	WOULD DATE	GIRL FRIEND	ENGAGED
beautiful	67.33	46.50	37.07	33.37
good cook	82.58	68.39	58.67	59.50
kind	63.33	61.00	45.33	45.00
youth	76.83	49.06	57.19	39.60
love	69.67	39.67	22.73	27.00
honest	8187	64.67	46.77	50.00
FEMALE SAMPLE	JUST MET	WOULD DATE	BOY FRIEND	ENGAGED
love	79.39	32.90	18.70	19.70
wealthy	80.82	66.70	63.70	60.60
fun	69.20	29.30	21.70	30.20
honest	80.94	67.10	57.00	47.50
sportsman	75.31	64.30	55.20	62.00
employed	75.42	75.00	69.90	45.51
kind	79.69	55.20	46.88	46.50
happy	79.48	31.00	20.50	20.30
COMBINED SAMPLE	JUST MET	WOULD DATE	BOY/GIRL FRIEND	ENGAGED
kind	73.48	57.41	46.28	45.94
love	75.70	35.44	20.21	22.44
honest	81.29	66.19	53.09	48.46

Table 6.6 Z-scores of Difference Between Subsequent Levels
on Distances From Attributes: Japanese Sample

MALE SAMPLE	JUST MET and WOULD DATE	WOULD DATE and GIRLFRIEND	GIRLFRIEND and ENGAGED
beautiful	1.88	1.07	0.50
good cook	1.16	0.90	0.20
kind	0.83	1.24	0.20
youth	3.06*	0.26	0.17
love	2.69*	2.34*	0.21
honest	2.18*	1.72	0.31
FEMALE SAMPLE	JUST MET and WOULD DATE	WOULD DATE and BOYFRIEND	BOYFRIEND and ENGAGED
love	6.06*	2.15*	0.22
wealthy	2.08*	0.79	0.45
fun	5.78*	0.91	1.01
honest	1.84	1.84	1.37
sportsman	1.37	0.85	0.57
employed	0.80	0.90	3.71*
kind	2.01*	0.68	0.60
happy	6.06*	1.92	0.65
COMBINED SAMPLE	JUST MET and WOULD DATE	WOULD DATE and BOY/GIRLFRIEND	BOY/GIRLFRIEND and ENGAGED
kind	2.22*	1.37	0.62
love	6.71*	3.23*	0.32
honest	2.97*	2.63*	1.24

*p<.05

in an attribute between these two levels distinguishes the mate relationship from the social acquaintance relationship. In other words, this first stage might be said to represent the field of availables. The transition between SOMEONE YOU WOULD DATE and boy/girlfriend is the juncture at which a dating relationship becomes exclusive—the point at which the field is cleared (Cushman and Cahn 1985). Finally, the transition between BOY/GIRLFRIEND and SOMEONE YOU WOULD BE ENGAGED TO is one of making a commitment. It is at this juncture that the couple has publicly declared an intent to permanently commit to one another as mates. This four stage sequence is actually a three stage sequence of mateship, preceded by a pre-mate phase.

Table 6.5 shows that the attributes are progressively closer to more intimate mateship levels, indicating that each is an important characteristic of the mate relationship. The more important analysis, however, appears in Table 6.6, which shows whether these mean distances become significantly closer to higher mateship levels. Those that do not can be labelled entry variables; those that do can be labelled intensity variables.

The z-scores in Table 6.6 indicate that for the male sample, five attributes are neither significantly closer to GIRLFRIEND than to SOMEONE YOU WOULD DATE,, *nor are they* significantly closer to ENGAGED than to SOMEONE YOU WOULD DATE. Hence, these attributes operate as entry variables: BEAUTIFUL, GOOD COOK, KIND, YOUTH, and HONEST. Of these variables, two are significantly closer to SOMEONE YOU WOULD DATE than to SOMEONE YOU JUST MET, sharply differentiating the social acquaintance relationship from the mate relationship: YOUTH and HONEST.

No intensity variables can be identified for the male sample. However, LOVE operates as a marker variable (as defined in Chapter Two). LOVE is significant at the first two steps in the sequence but not at the third. In other words, for males, LOVE differentiates SOMEONE YOU JUST MET from SOMEONE YOU WOULD DATE and SOMEONE YOU WOULD DATE from GIRLFRIEND, but it does not differentiate GIRLFRIEND from SOMEONE YOU WOULD BE ENGAGED TO. The juncture at which LOVE becomes significantly closer is the point of "clearing the field." Once the field has been cleared, LOVE operates similarly to entry variables. For males, LOVE seems to mark the point at which the pair clears the field to become a couple.

For females, six attributes are neither significantly closer to BOYFRIEND than to SOMEONE YOU WOULD DATE, *nor are they* significantly closer to ENGAGED than to SOMEONE YOU WOULD DATE. Hence, these attributes operate as entry variables: WEALTHY, FUN, HONEST, SPORTSMAN, KIND, and HAPPY. Of these variables, four are significantly closer to SOMEONE YOU WOULD DATE than to SOMEONE YOU JUST MET, sharply differentiating the social acquaintance relationship from the mate relationship: WEALTHY, FUN, KIND, and HAPPY.

No traditional intensity variables can be identified for the female sample either. However, EMPLOYED can be labelled a commitment-intensity variable (as defined in Chapter Two). EMPLOYED is not significantly closer to BOYFRIEND than to SOMEONE YOU WOULD DATE, but it is significantly closer to SOMEONE YOU WOULD BE ENGAGED TO. The juncture at which EMPLOYED becomes significantly closer is the point of public declaration of commitment to one another as mates. Clearly, financial security is of utmost importance to the females in this sample.

Finally, as for the male sample, LOVE operates as a marker variable. LOVE is significant at the first two steps in the sequence but not at the third. The juncture at which LOVE becomes significantly closer is the point of "clearing the field." Once the field has been cleared, LOVE operates similarly to entry variables. For females as well as males, LOVE seems to mark the point at which the pair clears the field to become a couple.

The other two variables that are common to males and females are HONEST and KIND. Although both are labelled as entry variables for males and females alike, they operate slightly differently for the two groups. For females, KIND differentiates SOMEONE YOU JUST MET from SOMEONE YOU WOULD DATE, showing a sharp distinction on this variable for entry into the mate relationship. There is no such distinction for males. Conversely, for males, HONEST differentiates SOMEONE YOU JUST MET from SOMEONE YOU WOULD DATE, showing a sharp distinction on this variable for entry into the mate relationship. There is no such distinction for females.

Conclusion

A comparison of Table 6.1 with Ju's (in Nicotera and Associates

1993) results summarized in the introduction to this chapter reveals considerable agreement. Recall that Ju's respondents were asked to choose the three most important mateship attributes from a list of eleven traditionally valued characteristics. The attributes were then rank ordered according to the percentage of the sample that selected each attribute as one of their three choices: Love (64.4 percent), Emotional Compatibility (53.8 percent); High Moral Standards (46.0 percent); Work Ability (35.4 percent); Occupation (22.6 percent); Family Financial Condition (21.5 percent); Common Interest (21.1 percent); Age (6.8 percent); Education (6.4 percent); Looks (4.3 percent); and Family Social Position (2.7 percent). In the present study, only two of these were not mentioned at all by either male or female respondents: Emotional Compatibility and Common Interests (although the latter is difficult to judge without knowing the particular interests of the respondents). For females, two additional attributes were not mentioned: High Moral Standards and Occupation. For both males and females, EMPLOYED is similar to Work Ability and WEALTH to Family Financial Condition. In addition, for males, GOOD CHARACTER is similar to High Moral Standards and ONLY HOUSEWIFE to Occupation. From those considered to be most salient (and therefore pursued in the present study) several occur that are not considered to be traditionally valued, according to Ju (in Nicotera and Associates 1993). These are KIND and HONEST for all participants, adding GOOD COOK for males and FUN, SPORTS-MAN, and HAPPY for females. HONEST may be a specific attribute subsumed under High Moral Standards. The results of this study show that Japanese youth still value highly some of the traditional mateship attributes identified by Ju. However, they value others less and have developed new, more materialistic values for a mate.

Focusing on the results of the present study, the list of attributes generated by the open-ended survey and facilitated discussion show that for Japanese males, an ideal mate is characterized by her beauty, cooking ability, kindness, youth, love, and honesty. For Japanese females, an ideal mate is characterized by his love, wealth, being fun, honesty, being a sportsman, employment, kindness, and happiness. These lists make for an interesting comparison of gender-linked values. For males, physical attractiveness topped the list (65 percent); for females it was mentioned by only 15 percent of the sample, not reaching the 30 percent criterion for inclusion in the second survey. Conversely, love was number one on the females' list, mentioned by 85 percent of the female respondents; on the males' list love ranks fifth, with only 40 percent of male respondents even mentioning it. Still, lest a value judgement be made that Japanese females are less materialistic, note that wealthy (75 percent) is second on their list, as compared to 20 percent of males mentioning it, not enough to be included in the second survey. It is clear that the decision to treat males and females as separate samples was warranted, especially given the results for entry and intensity variable analysis, discussed below.

The mateship levels that were identified in this study are identical for males and females and are quite similar in character to past U.S. research in this tradition (casual date, steady date, fiancee, and spouse). Qualitatively and statistically, the mate relationship progresses through the following stages: first meeting, dating, boy/girlfriend, and engagement.

The one functional difference between the traditional U.S. labels (casual date, steady date, fiancee, and spouse) and the labels found for Japanese students in this study is that data from this study did not specify a marriage stage; however, it is presumed that marriage follows engagement. What is interesting is that respondents did not seem to perceive "marriage" as qualitatively different enough from "engaged" to warrant listing it. It seems that once the mateship commitment is made public, through engagement, the bond is sealed.

The nature of the attributes as entry or intensity variables is another interesting set of analyses. For males, five entry variables are identified: Beautiful, good cook, kind, youth, and honest—youth and honest sharply differentiating the social acquaintance relationship from the mate relationship. For females, six attributes are identified as entry variables: Wealthy, fun, honest, sportsman, kind, and happy—wealthy, fun, kind, and happy sharply differentiating the social acquaintance relationship from the mate relationship.

Although no traditional intensity variables were identified for either females or males, love is identified as a marker variable for both sexes, differentiating the social acquaintance relationship from the budding mate relationship and then significantly increasing to the point of "clearing the field." For Japanese culture, love marks the point at which the pair becomes a couple.

Finally, for Japanese females, "employed" was labelled a commitment-intensity variable becoming significant at the point of making the transition to engagement. Again, financial security seems to be of utmost importance to the females in this sample.

Besides love, honest and kind are common to males and females. Although both are labelled as entry variables for males and females alike, they operate slightly differently for the two groups. For females only, "kind" sharply differentiates the social acquaintance relationship from the beginning mate relationship; whereas "honest" operates in this way only for males.

This study has revealed an overall pattern of mate relationship development for Japanese culture, while at the same time demonstrating different processes for females and males. In addition, the general structure of the theory is supported, and the general methodology has been once again shown to be fruitful.

CHAPTER SEVEN

CONFLICT AND RELATIONAL DISINTEGRATION

In the first chapter, several propositions (see also Nicotera and Associates 1993) for interpersonal relationships were presented. This chapter presents explorations of Proposition 5 for White Americans of European descent, African Americans, White Deaf Americans of European descent, and Jamaicans. Proposition 5 states that conflict that threatens self-concept support on crucial relationship variables—the lack of it or attacks on it—is potentially the most dangerous type of conflict in interpersonal relationships. As reported in Nicotera and Associates (1993), the logic of this proposition is supported by a variety of research. The validity of this proposition is directly explored with two research questions.

RQ3a: Is the absence of self concept support on crucial relationship variables related to relational disintegration?

RQ3b: What are potential sources of conflict for each level of mate relationships and for mate relationships in general?

Given the exploratory nature of this research and problems with translation, these RQs are applied only to the cultures studied in English-speaking countries (i.e., American co-cultures and Jamaica, but not Japan). Also because of the exploratory nature of the questions, the term "relational disintegration" in RQ3a was operationalized as simply "breaking up." Although this is a rather rough definition, it does get to the most extreme form of disintegration—the total demise of the relationship. In addition, it is an unequivocal vernacular term that respondents can easily identify and relate to. Results from the present analysis will allow insight into the viability of the proposition that lack of support on crucial relationship attributes leads to relational disintegration. Future study can then more deeply explore the intricate processes of such disintegration, and consider how our exploration of this process fits into the overall literature on relational disintegration.

Procedures

As part of the open-ended survey in the first stage of data collection (described in full in previous chapters), participants (except for those in Japan) were asked to list several sources (topics) of conflict in mate relationships. As with attributes and levels, the most commonly mentioned of these were used to construct part of the second survey. For the second stage of data collection, the relationship levels (see the appropriate chapter for each culture) were arrayed in the Galileo questionnaire in paired comparisons of the concept "breaking up" with "lack of" each attribute (RQ3a); and conflict sources with levels (RQ3b). Following all the paired comparisons was a set of questions asking what "things could cause conflict" for each of the relationship stages (RQ3b). (See the appropriate chapter for each cultural group for a description of the samples.)

Analysis

Research Question 3a assesses whether a lack of the attributes discovered in RQ1 (see appropriate chapter for each culture) is related to relational disintegration. To explore this RQ, mean distances between the "lack of" each attribute and the concept "breaking up" were examined. RQ3b seeks to identify sources of conflict for each level (see appropriate chapter for each culture) and for mate relationships in general. First, the list of conflict sources from the first survey were analyzed to create a list of those mentioned by at least 30 percent of the sample. Mean distances were examined between these conflict sources and the levels, as decided upon after quantitative analysis of Galileo data on levels (see appropriate chapter for each culture). Finally, the open-ended question in the second survey elicited further sources, specific to each level.

Results and Interpretations: White Americans

The mateship attributes identified as crucial for White Americans of European descent are TRUST, FRIENDSHIP, LOVE, HONESTY, COMMUNICATION, CARING, LOYALTY, AFFECTION, PHYSICAL ATTRACTIVENESS, RESPECT, INTELLIGENCE, SUPPORT, and SEXUAL ATTRACTION. Research Question 3a assesses whether a lack of these attributes is related to relational disintegration. To explore this RQ, mean distances between the "lack of" each attribute and the concept "breaking up" were examined. Table 7.1 contains the results of these tests, arrayed in order such that those attributes closest to BREAKING UP are at the top of the list. Results for FRIENDSHIP could not be obtained due to excessive missing data.

Table 7.1 Mean Distances Between "Lack of" Attributes and "Breaking up" for White Americans

LACK OF...	MEAN DIST.	TYPE
love	10.00	C-I
trust	11.04	I
caring	11.33	I
loyalty	11.79	M
honesty	12.00	I
communication	14.330	M
respect	17.42	E
support	18.71	I
affection	21.96	I
sexual attractiveness	29.29	M
phys. attractiveness	29.75	E
intelligence	32.33	I
friendship	missing data	

As shown by the table, the attributes' order of importance for relational maintenance (defined roughly as staying together) is LOVE, TRUST, CARING, LOYALTY, HONESTY, COMMUNICATION, RESPECT,

SUPPORT, AFFECTION, SEXUAL ATTRACTION, PHYSICAL ATTRACTION, and INTELLIGENCE. In addition, the mean distances from BREAKING UP are rather small, indicating close associations between the concepts. There does not seem to be a relationship between maintenance and the status of each attribute as an entry, intensity, commitment-intensity, or marker variable, as there is no discernable pattern regarding this feature. Note, however, that the six traditional variables that were added to the analysis for Chapter Two (even though they did not meet the 30 percent criterion for inclusion) have the farthest distance from BREAKING UP and may be interpreted as having the least amount of importance for relational maintenance of all the attributes. This may indicate that these traditional variables are not crucial after all. If we eliminate these from consideration, it seems that intensity variables are more important for relational maintenance than entry or marker variables.

Z-scores of the difference were computed between each possible pair of attributes to see if they were significantly different regarding their distance from "breaking up." Several significant differences were found for two of the traditional variables, physical attractiveness and sexual appeal. PHYSICAL ATTRACTIVENESS is significantly ($p<.05$) less important for maintenance than LOVE ($z=2.70$), TRUST ($z=2.64$), CARING ($z=2.59$), LOYALTY ($z=2.76$), HONESTY ($z=2.43$), and COMMUNICATION ($z=2.18$). SEXUAL ATTRACTION is significantly less important for maintenance than LOVE ($z=2.80$), TRUST ($z=2.73$), CARING ($z=2.69$), LOYALTY ($z=2.86$), HONESTY ($z=2.53$), COMMUNICATION ($z=2.27$), and RESPECT ($z=1.96$).

Research Question 3b seeks to identify sources of conflict for each level and for mate relationships in general. First, the list of conflict sources from the first survey were analyzed to create a list of those mentioned by at least 30 percent of the sample. The resulting list of conflict sources is: JEALOUSY, OTHER FRIENDS (one partner not liking or disapproving of the other's friends), MONEY, and TIME SPENT TOGETHER. Table 7.2 contains these results. Mean distances were examined between these conflict sources and the levels concluded from the analysis in Chapter Two (OCCASIONAL DATE, EXCLUSIVE DATE, and MARRIAGE). Table 7.3 contains those results. Finally, z-scores of difference were computed between mateship levels for their distances from the conflict sources. Table 7.4 contains those results.

Table 7.2 Sources of Conflict for White Americans

SOURCE OF CONFLICT	% MALE	% FEMALE	% TOTAL
jealousy	57	39	47
other friends	50	39	44
money	36	44	41
time spent together	36	28	31

Table 7.3 Mean Distances Between Sources of Conflict and Mateship Levels: White Americans

CONFLICT OVER...	OCC. DATE	EXC. DATE	MARRIAGE
jealousy	67.75	42.30	30.26
other friends	74.91	51.27	98.00
money	124.35	59.87	33.65
time spent together	80.95	39.45	26.14

Table 7.4 Z-scores of Difference Between Mateship Levels for Distances from Conflict Sources: White Americans

	OCCASIONAL DATE and EXCLUSIVE DATE	EXCLUSIVE DATE and MARRIAGE	OVERALL: OCC. DATE and MARRIAGE
jealousy	1.41	2.26*	3.00*
other friends	0.86	0.25	0.85
money	1.24	1.67	2.83*
time spent together	1.6	1.81	3.07*

*$p<.05$

Table 7.3 shows a similar pattern for conflict over JEALOUSY, MONEY, and TIME TOGETHER; these things seem to be increasingly a source of conflict as mateship level increases. Table 7.4 shows that overall, all three of these conflict sources are significantly closer to

MARRIAGE than to OCCASIONAL DATE. We may conclude that jealousy, money, and time spent together are significant sources of conflict in the mate relationship. The pattern for conflict over OTHER FRIENDS is uneven, and Table 7.4 shows that it is not significantly different for different levels of relationship. Although it was salient to the respondents, it does not seem to be important in the scheme of relational development.

Finally, an open-ended question in the second survey elicited further sources of conflict, specific to each level. The sample generated sixteen different sources of conflict for the level OCCASIONAL DATE, eighteen for EXCLUSIVE DATE, and twenty-eight for MARRIAGE. Table 7.5 contains these results.

Table 7.5 Sources of Conflict by Mateship Levels for White Americans

OCCASIONAL DATE	% M	% F	% TOT	EXCLUSIVE DATE	% M	% F	% TOT
communication	33	7	14	**communication**	17	20	19
respect	0	20	14	**trust**	33	13	19
different interests	0	13	10	**honesty**	0	20	14
honesty	0	13	10	**infidelity**	0	20	14
anything	0	7	5	**dating others**	17	7	10
dating others	0	7	5	**jealousy**	17	7	10
different interests	17	0	5	**time**	0	13	10
incompatible	0	7	5	caring	17	0	5
miscommunication	17	0	5	commitment pressure	0	7	5
money	0	7	5				
nothing	0	7	5	doubts	0	7	5
phys. attractiveness	0	7	5	intolerance	17	0	5
stops calling	17	0	5	love	17	0	5
time	0	7	5	loyalty	0	7	5
time together	17	0	5	money	0	7	5
trust	0	7	5	selfishness	17	0	5
				stubbornness	17	0	5
				too close	17	0	5
				understanding	17	0	5

(Table 7.5 cont.)

MARRIAGE	% M	% F	% TOT	MARRIAGE (CONT.)	% M	% F	% TOT
money	17	40	33	family	0	7	5
infidelity	17	20	19	friends	0	7	5
kids	17	20	19	humor	17	0	5
communication	0	2	14	jealousy	0	7	5
trust	17	13	14	loyalty	0	7	5
affection	17	7	10	personal growth	0	7	5
honesty	0	13	10	personal habits	0	7	5
love	17	7	10	religion	17	0	5
time	0	13	10	responsibility changes	0	7	5
betrayal	0	7	5	secrets	0	7	5
boredom	17	0	5	self esteem lack	0	7	5
caring	17	0	5	sex	17	0	5
commitment	0	7	5	support	0	7	5
different interests	0	7	5	work	0	7	5

Several respondents left this page of the survey blank; percentages are based on the total number of responses to this set of questions. All conflict sources mentioned are included in the table. Those in bold are the ones that were mentioned by more than one respondent. Positive words (i.e., honesty and trust) were phrased in the negative ("lack of" or dishonesty, distrust, etc.). For inclusion in the table, such negative phrasing was reworded so that similarities between this set of lists and the list of crucial relationship attributes could be highlighted. Along with several other factors, many of the crucial variables are mentioned as conflict sources. Respondents were allowed to list as many sources of conflict as they liked for each level.

It is interesting to note that respondents perceived many more sources of conflict at the deeper relationship stages than at earlier stages. This pattern persisted throughout the individual responses and, as will be discussed later, throughout responses of the other cultural groups as well.

Results and Interpretation: African Americans

The mateship attributes identified as crucial for African Americans are HONESTY, COMMUNICATION, LOVE, CARING, PATIENCE, TRUST, UNDERSTANDING, INTELLIGENT, RESPECT, PHYSICALLY ATTRACTIVE, SEXUALLY APPEALING, AFFECTION, and SUPPORT. As for the White American study, the latter six are the traditional variables that were mentioned but did not meet the 30 percent criterion. Research Question 3a assesses whether a lack of these attributes is related to relational disintegration. To explore this RQ, mean distances between the "lack of" each attribute and the concept "breaking up" were examined. Table 7.6 contains the results of these tests, arrayed in order such that those attributes closest to BREAKING UP are at the top of the list.

As shown by the table, the attributes' order of importance for relational maintenance (defined roughly as staying together) is TRUST, RESPECT, UNDERSTANDING, HONESTY, COMMUNICATION, CARING, LOVE, PATIENCE, SUPPORT, AFFECTION, SEXUALLY APPEALING, PHYSICALLY

Table 7.6 Mean Distances Between "Lack of" Attributes and "Breaking up" for African Americans

LACK OF...	MEAN DIST.	TYPE
trust	8.60	I
respect	9.55	I
understanding	10.83	I
honesty	12.26	I
communication	13.64	I
caring	15.21	I
love	15.43	I
patience	22.71	I
support	23.86	I
affection	28.74	I
sexual appeal	58.68	E
phys. attractiveness	80.68	E
intelligence	98.60	E

ATTRACTIVE, and INTELLIGENT. Intensity variables seem to be most important for relational maintenance. In addition, the mean distances from BREAKING UP are rather small, indicating close associations between the concepts. Except for RESPECT, the traditional variables that were added to the analysis for Chapter Three (even though they did not meet the 30 percent criterion for inclusion) have the farthest distance from BREAKING UP and may be interpreted as having the least amount of importance for relational maintenance of all the attributes. As with the White sample, this may indicate that these traditional variables are not crucial at all.

Z-scores of the difference were computed between each possible pair of attributes to see if they were significantly different regarding their distance from "breaking up." Numerous significant differences were found. The differences are concentrated around the traditional crucial variables, except for RESPECT. Only one difference occurred that did not involve the traditional variables; PATIENCE is significantly less important than TRUST ($z=2.02$).

The traditional entry variables, SEXUALLY APPEALING, PHYSICALLY ATTRACTIVE, and INTELLIGENT, are the three least important attributes for maintenance and are significantly less important ($p<.05$) for maintenance than all the others on the list. Specifically, SEXUALLY APPEALING is significantly less important for maintenance than TRUST ($z=6.02$), RESPECT ($z=5.64$), UNDERSTANDING ($z=5.03$), HONESTY ($z=4.93$), COMMUNICATION ($z=4.90$), CARING ($z=4.78$), LOVE ($z=4.60$), PATIENCE ($z=3.30$), SUPPORT ($z=2.52$), and AFFECTION ($z=2.28$). PHYSICALLY ATTRACTIVE is significantly less important for maintenance than TRUST ($z=8.58$), RESPECT ($z=8.06$), UNDERSTANDING ($z=7.29$), HONESTY ($z=7.12$), COMMUNICATION ($z=7.01$), CARING ($z=6.83$), LOVE ($z=6.57$), PATIENCE ($z=4.99$), SUPPORT ($z=4.21$), and AFFECTION ($z=3.87$). INTELLIGENT is significantly less important for maintenance than TRUST ($z=7.11$), RESPECT ($z=6.71$), UNDERSTANDING ($z=6.10$), HONESTY ($z=5.98$), COMMU-NICATION ($z=5.93$), CARING ($z=5.80$), LOVE ($z=5.61$), PATIENCE ($z=4.28$), SUPPORT ($z=3.54$), and AFFECTION ($z=3.28$).

The traditional intensity variables, AFFECTION and SUPPORT, are the next least important attributes for maintenance and are significantly ($p<.05$) less important for maintenance than several above them on the list. Specifically, AFFECTION is significantly less important than TRUST ($z=3.18$), RESPECT ($z=2.86$), UNDERSTANDING ($z=2.35$), HONESTY ($z=2.29$), COMMUNICATION ($z=2.31$), CARING ($z=2.23$), and

LOVE (z=2.10). SUPPORT is significantly less important than TRUST (z=3.11), RESPECT (z=2.78), UNDERSTANDING (z=2.25), HONESTY (z=2.19), COMMUNICATION (z=2.21), CARING (z=2.13), and LOVE (z=2.10).

Table 7.7 Sources of Conflict for African Americans

SOURCE OF CONFLICT	% MALE	% FEMALE	% TOTAL
jealousy	67	54	58
time spent together	33	46	42
other friends	33	38	37
money	50	31	37

Table 7.8 Mean Distances Between Sources of Conflict and Mateship Levels: African Americans

SOURCE OF CONFLICT	DATING	ENGAGED	MARRIAGE
jealousy	100.20	2967.38	7241.67
time spent together	66.52	284.84	2379.77
other friends	123.90	331.24	2745.59
money	2521.07	2870.91	4951.30

Table 7.9 Z-scores of Difference Between Mateship Levels for Distances from Conflict Sources: African Americans

	DATING and ENGAGED	ENGAGED and MARRIAGE	OVERALL: DATING and MARRIAGE
jealousy	1.19	0.9	1.76
time spent together	0.93	0.89	0.98
other friends	0.84	0.97	1.06
money	0.10	0.51	0.59

*p<.05

Research Question 3b seeks to identify sources of conflict for each level and for mate relationships in general. First, the list of conflict sources from the first survey were analyzed to create a list of those mentioned by at least 30 percent of the sample. The resulting list of conflict sources is: JEALOUSY, TIME SPENT TOGETHER, OTHER FRIENDS (one partner not liking or disapproving of the other's friends), and MONEY. This list is identical to the one generated from the data for White Americans, with the conflict sources in a different order of salience. Table 7.7 contains these results. Mean distances were examined between these conflict sources and the levels concluded from the analysis in Chapter Three (DATING, ENGAGED, and MARRIAGE). Table 7.8 contains those results. Finally, z-scores of difference were computed between mateship levels for their distances from the conflict sources. Table 7.9 contains those results.

Table 7.8 shows a pattern for all sources of conflict, which is distinctly different from the White sample; these things seem to be *decreasingly* a source of conflict as mateship level increases. Table 7.9 shows that overall, none of these conflict sources are significantly closer to subsequent mateship levels. Especially given the large numbers, we may conclude that jealousy, time spent together, other friends, and money are not significant sources of conflict in the mate relationship for African Americans. Although these sources of conflict were reported as salient by the respondents, they do not seem to be important in the scheme of relational development.

Finally, an open-ended question in the second survey elicited further sources of conflict, specific to each level. The sample generated thirty-nine different sources of conflict for the level DATING, forty-one for ENGAGED, and fifty-one for MARRIAGE. Table 7.10 contains these results.

Table 7.10 Sources of Conflict by Mateship Level: African Americans

DATING	% M	% F	% TOT	ENGAGED	% M	% F	% TOT
honesty	13	47	40	communication	38	38	38
commitment	13	21	19	honesty	0	44	36
communication	88	3	19	trust	25	32	31
respect	25	18	19	commitment	13	21	19
time	25	15	17	money	0	21	17
jealousy	0	15	12	respect	0	18	14
infidelity	13	6	7	time	13	15	14
personality	13	6	7	infidelity	38	6	12
trust	0	9	7	family	13	6	7
attraction	13	3	5	past	13	6	7
different views	13	3	5	phys. attractiveness	0	9	7
friends	13	3	5	sex appeal	0	9	7
interest	13	3	5	understanding	0	9	7
money	0	6	5	caring	0	6	5
others	0	6	5	doubts/concerns	0	6	5
sex appeal	0	6	5	support	0	6	5
anything	0	3	2	abuse	0	3	2
attractiveness	0	3	2	affection	0	3	2
battery	0	3	2	appreciation	0	3	2
caring	0	3	2	attraction	0	3	2
common ideals	0	3	2	betrayal	13	0	2
courtesy	13	0	2	character change	0	3	2
differences in bkgrd.	0	3	2	cohabitation	0	3	2
different desires	0	3	2	common goals	0	3	2
growth	0	3	2	different views	0	3	2
hidden agenda	13	0	2	distance	0	3	2
humor	0	3	2	fear	0	3	2
intimacy	13	0	2	friends	13	0	2
misconception	13	0	2	future plans	0	3	2

(Table 7.10 cont.)

DATING (cont.)	% M	% F	% TOT	ENGAGED (cont.)	% M	% F	% TOT
misunderstanding	0	3	2	humor	0	3	2
neglect	0	3	2	in-laws	0	3	2
other dates	0	3	2	intimacy	0	3	2
patience	0	3	2	jealousy	0	3	2
phys. attractiveness	0	3	2	love	0	3	2
possessiveness	0	3	2	loyalty	0	3	2
selfishness	0	3	2	misunderstanding	0	3	2
sex	0	3	2	openness	0	3	2
sexual pressure	0	3	2	others	0	3	2
transportation	0	3	2	patience	0	3	2
				pressure	0	3	2
				sex	0	3	2

MARRIAGE	% M	% F	% TOT	MARRIAGE (cont.)	% M	% F	% TOT
communication	50	47	48	**support**	0	9	7
money	38	47	45	**understanding**	0	9	7
honesty	25	41	38	**caring**	0	6	5
trust	13	35	31	**humor**	13	6	5
respect	13	24	21	**in-laws**	0	6	5
infidelity	25	18	19	**patience**	0	6	5
kids	13	21	19	abuse	0	3	2
time	13	21	19	activity	0	3	2
love	13	15	14	attraction	0	3	2
sex	25	9	12	awareness	0	3	2
phys. attractiveness	0	12	10	betrayal	13	0	2
sex appeal	0	12	10	character change	0	3	2
affection	13	3	7	creativity	0	3	2
commitment	0	9	7	differing viewpoints	0	3	2
family	0	9	7	doubts	0	3	2

(Table 7.10 cont.)

Marriage (cont.)	% M	% F	% TOT	Marriage (cont.)	% M	% F	% TOT
drinking	0	3	2	misunderstandings	0	3	2
focus	0	3	2	others	0	3	2
friends	0	3	2	pressure	0	3	2
grow separately	0	3	2	relatives	0	3	2
household issues	13	0	2	sensitivity	0	3	2
incompatible	0	3	2	smoking	0	3	2
interest (lose)	0	3	2	stress	0	3	2
intimacy	0	3	2	thoughtfulness	0	3	2
jealousy	0	3	2	too much time together	0	3	2
living habits	0	3	2	work	13	0	2
loyalty	0	3	2				

A few respondents left this page of the survey blank; percentages are based on the total number of responses to this set of questions. All conflict sources mentioned are included in the table. Those in bold are the ones that were mentioned by more than one respondent. As for the White American sample, positive words (i.e., honesty and trust) were phrased in the negative ("lack of" or dishonesty, distrust, etc.). Again, for inclusion in the table, such negative phrasing was reworded so that similarities between this set of lists and the list of crucial relationship attributes could be highlighted. Quite similar to the results for the White American sample, many of the crucial variables are mentioned as conflict sources. Recall that respondents were allowed to list as many sources of conflict as they liked for each level. These respondents also perceived many more sources of conflict at the deeper relationship stages than at earlier stages. This pattern persisted throughout the individual responses.

Results and Interpretations: Deaf White Americans

The mateship attributes identified as crucial for Deaf White Americans of European descent are FUN, COMMUNICATION, HONESTY, LOVE, AFFECTION, SUPPORT, SEXUAL ATTRACTION, TRUST, FRIENDSHIP, and RESPECT. Research Question 3a assesses whether a lack of these attributes is related to relational disintegration. To explore this RQ, mean distances between the "lack of" each attribute and the concept "breaking up" were examined. Table 7.11 contains the results of these tests, arrayed in order such that those attributes closest to BREAKING UP are at the top of the list. Results for FRIEND-SHIP could not be obtained due to excessive missing data. Since this same phenomenon occurred in the White hearing sample, it may be that respondents could not make sense of a "lack of friend-ship" being related to "breaking up" and so left this response item blank. Friendship may be too ambiguous a term, as it refers not only to a feature of the mate relationship but to a variety of other personal relationships in one's life.

Table 7.11   Mean Distances Between "Lack of" Attributes and "Breaking up" for Deaf White Americans

LACK OF...	MEAN DIST.
trust	14.71
respect	17.29
communication	21.25
love	22.50
honesty	25.83
affection	31.67
support	35.00
fun	71.04
sexual affection	75.20

As shown by the table, the attributes' order of importance for rela-tional maintenance (defined roughly as staying together) is TRUST, RESPECT, COMMUNICATION, LOVE, HONESTY, AFFECTION, SUPPORT, FUN, and SEXUAL ATTRACTION. Recall that the data for mateship levels in Chapter Four was inconclusive; therefore, it cannot be examined whether there is a relationship between the status of each attribute as an entry or intensity variable. Note, however, that sexual attraction is the farthest from BREAKING UP (like the previous two cultural groups) even though for this sample it did meet the 30 percent criterion for inclusion (unlike the previous groups). However, for this sample, all the attributes are equally important maintenance variables; no significant z-scores of the difference resulted in the tests between each possible pair of attributes to see if they were significantly different regarding their distance from BREAKING UP. As discussed in Chapter Four, however, Galileo data from this sample must be considered inconclusive.

Research Question 3b seeks to identify sources of conflict for each level and for mate relationships in general. First, the list of conflict sources from the first survey were analyzed to create a list of those mentioned by at least 30 percent of the sample. The resulting list of conflict sources is: LACK OF COMMUNICATION, JEALOUSY, and MONEY. Table 7.12 contains these results. Mean distances were examined between these conflict sources and the levels concluded from the analysis in Chapter Four (CASUAL DATE and MARRIAGE). Table 7.13 contains those results. Finally, z-scores of difference were computed between mateship levels for their distances from the conflict sources. Table 7.14 contains those results.

Table 7.12 Sources of Conflict for Deaf White Americans

SOURCE OF CONFLICT	% MALE	% FEMALE	% TOTAL
lack of communication	50	53	42
jealousy	25	46	36
money	25	46	36

Table 7.13 Mean Distances Between Sources of Conflict and Mateship Levels: Deaf White Americans

SOURCE OF CONFLICT	CASUAL DATE	MARRIAGE
lack of communication	95.00	51.42
jealousy	122.17	121.74
money	492.00	633.75

Table 7.14 Z-scores of Difference Between
Mateship Levels for Distances from Conflict
Sources: Deaf White Americans

	CASUAL DATE and MARRIAGE
lack of communication	1.72
jealousy	0.01
money	0.28

*p<.05

Table 7.13 shows dissimilar patterns for the conflict sources. Table 7.14 shows that overall, none of these conflict sources are significantly closer to MARRIAGE than to CASUAL DATE. We cannot conclude whether lack of communication, jealousy, and money are significant sources of conflict in the mate relationship, especially given the inconclusive nature of the stages used for analysis. These three sources of conflict were reported to be salient by 30 percent of the first sample; however, so were the mateship stages, which also turned out to be statistically nonsignificant in the Galileo tests (see Chapter Four).

Table 7.15 Sources of Conflict by Mateship Level: Deaf White Americans

CASUAL DATE	% M	% F	% TOT	MARRIAGE	% M	% F	% TOT
communication	42	9	26	**money**	42	36	39
money	8	18	13	**infidelity**	17	36	26
nothing	17	9	13	**communication**	17	27	22
trust	8	18	13	**jobs**	8	36	22
incompatible	8	9	9	**kids**	25	18	22
				love	17	18	17
adjustments	0	9	4	**honesty**	8	18	13
commitment	0	9	4	**trust**	17	9	13
dating others	0	9	4	**commitment**	8	9	9
different beliefs	0	9	4	**support**	0	18	9

(Table 7.15 cont.)

CASUAL DATE (cont.)	% M	% F	% TOT	MARRIAGE (cont.)	% M	% F	% TOT
feelings not expressed	0	9	4	accidents	8	0	4
fun	8	0	4	affection	8	0	4
honesty	8	0	4	different religion	8	0	4
interest lack	0	9	4	independence	8	0	4
manners	8	0	4	living place	0	9	4
misunderstanding	8	0	4	phys. attractiveness	8	0	4
sex	8	0	4	respect	8	0	4
time	0	9	4	sex	0	9	4
				sex appeal	8	0	4
				space	8	0	4
				time	0	9	4

Finally, an open-ended question in the second survey elicited further sources of conflict, specific to each level. The sample generated seventeen sources of conflict for the level CASUAL DATE and twenty-one for MARRIAGE. Table 7.15 contains these results.

A great number of respondents left this page of the survey blank; percentages are based on the total number of responses to this set of questions. All conflict sources mentioned are included in the table. Those in bold are the ones that were mentioned by more than one respondent. Again, positive words (i.e., honesty and trust) were phrased in the negative ("lack of" or dishonesty, distrust, etc.). For inclusion in the table, such negative phrasing was reworded so that similarities between this set of lists and the list of crucial relationship attributes could be highlighted. Many of the crucial variables are mentioned as conflict sources. Again, recall that respondents were allowed to list as many sources of conflict as they liked for each level.

It is interesting to note that, once again in another cultural group, respondents perceived many more sources of conflict at the deeper relationship stage than at the earlier stage. This pattern persisted throughout the individual responses.

Results and Interpretation: Jamaica

The mateship attributes identified as crucial for Jamaicans are TRUST, LOVE, HONESTY, RESPECT, COMMUNICATION, UNDERSTANDING, CARING, FRIENDSHIP, AFFECTION, SHARING, SUPPORT, PHYSICALLY ATTRACTIVE, INTELLIGENCE, and SEXUALLY APPEALING. Research question 3a assesses whether a lack of these attributes is related to relational disintegration. To explore this RQ, mean distances between the "lack of" each attribute and the concept "breaking up" were examined. Table 7.16 contains the results of these tests, arrayed in order such that those attributes closest to BREAKING UP are at the top of the list. As with the two White European U.S. samples, results for FRIENDSHIP could not be obtained due to excessive missing data. It does indeed seem that, universally, respondents were not able to make sense of a "lack of friendship" being related to "breaking up" and so left this response item blank.

Table 7.16   Mean Distances Between "Lack of" Attributes and "Breaking up" for Jamaicans

LACK OF...	MEAN DIST.	TYPE
affection	28.42	I
trust	29.40	I
honesty	29.42	I
respect	29.50	I
love	30.62	I
sharing	31.28	I
understanding	31.69	I
communication	31.98	I
caring	33.07	I
sex appeal	44.59	I
support	49.52	I
intelligence	70.79	E
physical attractiveness	77.07	E
friendship	missing data	

As shown by the table, the attributes' order of importance for relational maintenance (defined roughly as staying together) is AFFECTION, TRUST, HONESTY, RESPECT, LOVE, SHARING, UNDERSTANDING, COMMUNICATION, CARING, SEX APPEAL, SUPPORT, INTELLIGENCE, and PHYSICAL ATTRACTIVENESS. In addition, the mean distances from BREAKING UP are rather small, indicating close associations between the concepts. There does seem to be a relationship between maintenance and the status of each attribute as an entry or intensity variable, as the entry variables are also the two lowest ranking attributes.

Z-scores of the difference were computed between each possible pair of attributes to see if they were significantly different regarding their distance from "breaking up." Several significant differences were found for the two lowest ranking traditional variables, intelligence and physical attractiveness. PHYSICAL ATTRACTIVENESS is significantly less important for maintenance than AFFECTION (z=3.25), TRUST (z=3.53), HONESTY (z=3.25), RESPECT (z=3.04), LOVE (z=3.25), UNDERSTANDING (z=2.24), COMMUNICATION (z=2.71), CARING (z=2.07), and SEX APPEAL (z=1.99). INTELLIGENCE is significantly (p<.05) less important for maintenance than AFFECTION (z=4.47), TRUST (z=4.70), HONESTY (z=4.41), RESPECT (z=4.28), LOVE (z = 4.37), SHARING (z=3.25), UNDERSTANDING (z=3.47), COMMUNICATION (z=3.85), CARING (z=3.31), SEX APPEAL (z=3.11), and SUPPORT (z=2.97).

Research Question 3b seeks to identify sources of conflict for each level and for mate relationships in general. First, the list of conflict sources from the first survey were analyzed to create a list of those mentioned by at least 30 percent of the sample. The resulting list of conflict sources is: JEALOUSY, INSECURITY, and COMMUNICATION. Table 7.17 contains these results. Mean distances were examined between these conflict sources and the levels concluded from the analysis in Chapter Five. Table 7.18 contains those results. Finally, z-scores of difference were computed between mateship levels for their distances from the conflict sources. Table 7.19 contains those results.

Table 7.18 shows a similar pattern for conflict over JEALOUSY, INSECURITY, and COMMUNICATION; these things seem to be increasingly a source of conflict as mateship level increases. Table 7.18 shows that overall, all three of these conflict sources are signifi-

Table 7.17   Sources of Conflict for Jamaicans

SOURCE OF CONFLICT	% MALE	% FEMALE	% TOTAL
jealousy	10	50	32
insecurity	30	33	32
communication	20	42	32

Table 7.18   Mean Distances Between Sources of Conflict and Mateship Levels: Jamaicans

SOURCE OF CONFLICT	DATING	L-T COUPLE	MARRIAGE
jealousy	81.59	45.66	43.76
insecurity	73.80	44.39	41.29
communication	53.38	37.82	31.39

Table 7.19   Z-scores of Difference Between Mateship Levels for Distances from Conflict Sources: Jamacians

	DATING and L-T COUPLE	DATING and MARRIAGE
jealousy	1.63	3.02*
insecurity	2.33*	2.96*
communication	2.46*	3.91*

*p<.05

cantly closer to MARRIAGE than to DATING. However, JEALOUSY is not significantly different for DATING and LONG-TERM COUPLE. (As would be expected, none of the sources of conflict differ for LONG-TERM COUPLE and MARRIAGE). We may conclude that insecurity and communication are significant sources of conflict in the mate relationship. The pattern for JEALOUSY is less clear; the institutionalization of the relationship seems to have some effect on this source of conflict.

Table 7.20 Sources of Conflict by Mateship Level: Jamaicans

DATING	% M	% F	% TOT	L-T COUPLE	% M	% F	%TOT
communication	31	19	22	trust	44	16	24
understanding	19	16	17	communication	19	21	20
trust	13	14	14	honesty	31	14	19
commitment	19	5	8	understanding	13	14	14
diff. opinions/views	0	12	8	cheating	0	16	12
honesty	0	12	8	commitment	13	12	12
respect	6	9	8	jealousy	0	16	12
different interests	6	7	7	sex	19	9	12
punctuality	6	7	7	time	6	14	12
lack of interest	13	2	5	boredom	6	7	7
jealousy	0	7	5	love	19	2	7
love	6	5	5	sharing	6	7	7
caring	0	5	3	insecurity	0	7	5
intelligence	0	5	3	interest lack	6	5	5
not knowing each other well	0	5	3	caring	0	5	3
phys. attractiveness	6	2	3	respect	0	5	3
				sex appeal	13	0	3
sex	0	5	3	support	0	5	3
attention	6	0	2	affection	6	0	2
cheating	6	0	2	attention	6	0	2
different expectations	0	2	2	appearance	0	2	2
expect too much	0	2	2	frustration	0	2	2
incompatibility	0	2	2	hypocrisy	0	2	2
lack of experience	0	2	2	intimacy lack	6	0	2
personal growth	0	2	2	marriage desire	6	0	2
sex appeal	0	2	2	physical abuse	0	2	2
sharing	0	2	2	selfishness	0	2	2
tactlessness	0	2	2	taking for granted	0	2	2
time lack	0	2	2	only one partner grows	0	2	2

(Table 7.20 cont.)

MARRIAGE	% M	% F	% TOT
sex	25	42	37
communication	38	30	32
time	13	35	29
cheating	13	26	22
trust	25	21	22
understanding	19	16	17
honesty	19	14	15
commitment	19	12	14
jealousy	0	16	12
affection	6	7	7
love	19	2	7
respect	0	9	7
sex appeal	13	5	7
support	13	5	7
caring	0	5	3
insecurity	0	5	3
only one partner grows	0	5	3
attention	6	0	2
betray confidence	6	0	2
boredom	6	0	2
consideration	0	2	2
different views	0	2	2
insecurity	0	2	2
intimacy	6	0	2
meanness	0	2	2
physical abuse	0	2	2
physical attractiveness	0	2	2
selfishness	0	2	2
sharing	0	2	2
trust	0	2	2

Finally, an open-ended question in the second survey elicited further sources of conflict, specific to each level. Table 7.20 contains these results. Only a few respondents left this page of the survey blank; percentages are based on the total number of responses to this set of questions. All conflict sources mentioned are included in the table. Those in bold are the ones that were mentioned by more than one respondent. Again, positive words (i.e., honesty and trust) were phrased in the negative ("lack of" or dishonesty, distrust, etc.). For inclusion in the table, such negative phrasing was reworded so that similarities between this set of lists and the list of crucial relationship attributes could be highlighted. All of the crucial variables are mentioned as conflict sources. (Recall that respondents were allowed to list as many sources of conflict as they liked for each level.)

It is interesting to note that, yet again in another cultural group, respondents perceived more sources of conflict at the deeper relationship stage than at the earlier stage. This pattern persisted throughout the individual responses.

Conclusions

Because of the inconclusive nature of the Galileo data for the Deaf White American sample, the only discussion of this group will be for the open-ended question on conflict sources. A comparison of the other three cultures (European Americans, African Americans, and Jamaicans) for relational maintenance is quite interesting. For relational maintenance (simply defined as not breaking up), the two American co-cultures have distinctly different patterns. The two most important differences are the different levels of importance placed on love and trust. For hearing European Americans, a lack of love is most closely related to breaking up. However, for African Americans a lack of trust is most closely related to breaking up; lack of love ranks seventh, preceded by lack of trust, respect, understanding, honesty, communication, and caring. Trust is not unimportant to European Americans; it ranks second. However, respect—second most important for African Americans—ranks seventh for European Americans. Obviously, respect is much more important to African Americans for relational maintenance than it is to European Americans. A comparison of

Tables 7.1 and 7.6 is quite revealing. Although these two cultures are quite similar in the crucial attributes themselves (to be discussed in Chapter Nine), the importance of these attributes for relational maintenance differs. This finding has important implications for interracial relationships; this subject will be discussed in Chapter Nine.

For relational maintenance (simply defined as not breaking up), Jamaican culture has yet another distinctly different pattern than the two American co-cultures. For Jamaicans, a lack of affection is most closely related to breaking up; lack of affection ranks ninth and tenth for European- and African Americans, respectively. Clearly, Jamaican culture values affection for relational maintenance more than the American cultures studied. Lack of respect ranks 4th for Jamaicans—much more similar to African Americans (second) than to European Americans (seventh). Lack of love is also more similar between Jamaicans (fifth) and African Americans (seventh) than between Jamaicans (fifth) and European Americans (first). Lack of understanding (which does not appear at all on the European American list) ranks much lower for Jamaicans (seventh) than for African Americans (third). Finally, lack of caring is much less important to Jamaicans (ninth) than to either American group (third for European Americans and sixth for African Americans). A comparison of Tables 7.1, 7.6, and 7.16 is quite interesting. Although these cultures are quite similar in the crucial attributes themselves (to be discussed in Chapter Nine), the importance of these attributes for relational maintenance differs. This finding has important implications for interracial relationships; this subject will be discussed in Chapter Nine.

It is also quite interesting to compare the three American co-cultures and Jamaican culture on their lists of conflict sources. All three groups generated quite similar and rather predictable sources of relational conflict (see Tables 7.5, 7.10, 7.15, and 7.20). Likewise, all groups generated longer lists for the more intimate relationship levels. The African American sample generated the longest overall list, due to the fact that there were a great deal more unique (mentioned by only one person) sources of conflict mentioned. There appears to be less intracultural homogeneity for this group than for the others in regard to sources of relational conflict. This may be due to the highly open and realistic nature of communication that typifies this culture as discussed by Martin, Hecht, and Larkey (1994) and by Kochman (1982). This cultural group does indeed seem to be more willing than their European American counterparts, or even their African-Jamaican counterparts, to freely express the negative aspects of life. Conversely, the Deaf European American group generated the shortest list. This may be due to a reticence in response because of language translation difficulties between English and ASL. Finally, the most striking difference between Jamaicans and all the American groups is the emphasis on personal growth by Jamaicans, particularly by females. In addition to deeper exploration of these findings, future research needs to consider cross-cultural differences in meanings for similar terminology; concepts such as "respect" may mean widely different things in different cultures.

CHAPTER EIGHT

MATE RELATIONSHIP QUALITY

This chapter brings us to the last of the propositions (presented in Chapter One) examined in this volume. Proposition 7 states that quality interpersonal relationships consist of intimacy, personal growth, and effective communication on the crucial relationship variables. As explained in Nicotera and Associates (1993), this proposition asserts that intimacy in general, personal growth in general, personal growth on crucial relationship variables, and good communication about crucial relationship variables are all related to overall relationship quality; the logic of this proposition is supported by the traditional mateship literature. The proposition is directly explored with the following RQs. As with Proposition 5, these RQs are applied only to the cultures studied in English-speaking countries (White Americans, African Americans, White Deaf Americans, and Jamaicans).

RQ4: Is relational quality related to intimacy, personal growth, and effective communication on the crucial relationship variables?

RQ5: Are there other factors that can be identified as important for relationship quality in different cultures?

Procedures

As part of the open-ended survey in the first stage of data collection (described in full in previous chapters), participants were asked to list attributes of the mate relationship. These results represent the

119

answers to RQ1. For the second stage of data collection, these attributes were arrayed in the Galileo questionnaire in paired comparisons of the concept "quality relationship" with "intimacy (generally)," with "personal growth in relation to" each attribute, and with "good communication about" each attribute (RQ4). As part of the first survey, respondents answered an open-ended question asking what "things represent a quality relationship" (RQ5). This was asked as part of the first survey so that any relevant results could be included in the Galileo survey. As will be described, respondents in every culture studied overwhelmingly repeated their original list of attributes as being features of a quality relationship; in fact, most respondents actually made a note that referred to their original list of attributes (e.g., "see my answer for question 1"). (See the appropriate chapter for each cultural group for a description of the samples.)

Analysis

Research Question 4 assesses whether relationship quality is related to intimacy in general, personal growth in general, personal growth in relation to crucial attributes (from RQ1), and good communication about crucial attributes (RQ1, see appropriate chapter for each culture). To explore this RQ, mean distances were examined between QUALITY RELATIONSHIP and: INTIMACY (GENERALLY); PERSONAL GROWTH (GENERALLY); PERSONAL GROWTH IN RELATION TO (each attribute); and, finally, GOOD COMMUNICATION ABOUT (each attribute). RQ5 seeks to determine whether other features of relationship quality can be discovered. This was explored with analysis of an open-ended question on the first survey.

Results and Interpretations: White Americans

The mean distance between QUALITY RELATIONSHIP and INTIMACY (GENERALLY) is 15.65; the mean distance between QUALITY RELATIONSHIP and PERSONAL GROWTH (GENERALLY) is 25.86. A z-score of the difference between these two variables shows that they are not significantly different regarding their respective distances from QUALITY RELATIONSHIP.

The mateship attributes identified as crucial for White Americans of European descent are TRUST, FRIENDSHIP, LOVE, HONESTY, COMMUNICATION, CARING, LOYALTY, AFFECTION, PHYSICAL ATTRACTIVENESS, RESPECT, INTELLIGENCE, SUPPORT, and SEXUAL ATTRACTION. The mean distances between QUALITY RELATIONSHIP and PERSONAL GROWTH IN RELATION TO (each attribute) are displayed in Table 8.1, arrayed such that those with the smallest distance (hence the most important variables) appear at the top of the list. As for the relational disintegration items (Chapter Seven), the items using the attribute FRIENDSHIP were left blank by a great majority of the sample; the Deaf and Jamaican groups again showed the same pattern. Analyses for these items were abandoned. It was concluded that since the survey instructions for the disintegration and quality items specifically directed respondents to focus on mate (dating, romantic) relationships, they did not know how to answer these questions. The term "friendship" seems to have confused the respondents when used for items other than the traditional paired comparison format preceded by traditional Galileo instructions which did not specifically ask participants to focus on the mate relationship.

Table 8.1 Mean Distances Between QUALITY RELATIONSHIP and PERSONAL GROWTH IN RELATION TO Crucial Variables: White Americans

PERSONAL GROWTH IN RELATION TO...	MEAN DIST.
communication	9.00
honesty	12.70
trust	12.78
love	13.61
loyalty	14.70
caring	14.83
affection	19.04
support	19.96
respect	20.35
sexual attraction	26.00
intelligence	26.26
physical attractiveness	38.74

For a QUALITY RELATIONSHIP, PERSONAL GROWTH IN RELATION TO the crucial attributes is important as follows, from most to least important, as indicated by mean distances from QUALITY RELATIONSHIP: COMMUNICATION, HONESTY, TRUST, LOVE, LOYALTY, CARING, AFFECTION, SUPPORT, RESPECT, SEXUAL ATTRACTION, INTELLIGENCE, and PHYSICAL ATTRACTIVENESS. Z-scores of the differences among these personal growth variables reveal that PERSONAL GROWTH IN RELATION TO PHYSICAL ATTRACTIVENESS is significantly less important (p<.05) than PERSONAL GROWTH IN RELATION TO: COMMUNICATION (z=3.24), HONESTY (z=2.01), TRUST (z=2.34), LOVE (z=2.05), LOYALTY (z=2.33), and CARING (z=2.20). In addition, PERSONAL GROWTH IN RELATION TO COMMUNICATION is significantly more important than PERSONAL GROWTH IN RELATION TO INTELLIGENCE (Z=2.73), SEXUAL ATTRACTION (z=2.33), or AFFECTION (z=2.15).

The mean distances between QUALITY RELATIONSHIP and GOOD COMMUNICATION ABOUT (each attribute) are displayed in Table 8.2, arrayed such that those with the smallest distance (hence the most important variables) appear at the top of the list.

Table 8.2 Mean Distances Between QUALITY RELATIONSHIP and GOOD COMMUNICATION ABOUT Crucial Variables: White Americans

GOOD COMMUNICATION ABOUT...	MEAN DIST.
caring	14.04
love	14.65
affection	15.86
trust	16.30
honesty	16.61
respect	17.57
loyalty	18.26
support	18.30
communication	20.30
sexual attraction	21.57
intelligence	26.35
physical attractiveness	35.04

Table 8.3   Indicators of Relationship Quality: White Amercians

QUALITY INDICATOR	% M	% F	% TOT		% M	% F	% TOT
trust	64	61	63	optimism	7	6	6
honesty	50	39	44	sacrifice	7	6	6
good communication	21	50	38	sharing	14	0	6
love	29	33	31	companionship	0	6	3
friendship	14	33	31	compromise	0	6	3
compatibility	7	22	16	put other first	0	6	3
respect	14	17	16	reassurance	0	6	3
mutual support	0	22	13	separateness	0	6	3
togetherness	7	17	13	comfortable	0	6	3
understanding	7	17	13	giving	0	6	3
happy to be with	0	17	9	helping	0	6	3
affection	7	11	9	humor	0	6	3
attraction	14	11	13	proximity	0	6	3
intimacy	7	11	9	religion	0	6	3
commitment	14	6	9	role clarity	0	6	3
loyalty	14	6	9	confidence	7	0	3
acceptance	0	17	9	determination	7	0	3
fun	0	11	6	equality	7	0	3
good sex	0	11	6	fascination	7	0	3
listening	0	11	6	interdependence	7	0	3
caring	7	6	6	reliability	7	0	3
fidelity	7	6	6				

For a QUALITY RELATIONSHIP, GOOD COMMUNICATION ABOUT these attributes is important as follows, from most to least important, as indicated by mean distances from QUALITY RELATIONSHIP: CARING, LOVE, AFFECTION, TRUST, HONESTY, ESPECT, LOYALTY, SUPPORT, COMMUNICATION, SEXUAL ATTRACTION, INTELLIGENCE, and PHYSICAL ATTRACTIVENESS. There are no significant differences between any of these GOOD COMMUNICATION variables as regards their mean distance from QUALITY RELATIONSHIP. All are of equal importance as shown by statistical tests.

Concerning RQ5, the relationship attributes generated for the first research question seem to be representative of relational quality as well. In response to the open-ended question, participants listed several relationship quality indicators, but the most frequently occurring on the list mirror the list of relationship attributes. In addition, more than half the sample (six males and twelve females) also directly referred to their original list of attributes. The results for this question are summarized in Table 8.3.

Results and Interpretations: African Americans

The mean distance between QUALITY RELATIONSHIP and INTIMACY (GENERALLY) is 23.08; the mean distance between QUALITY RELATIONSHIP and PERSONAL GROWTH (GENERALLY) is 28.42. A z-score of the difference between these two variables shows that they are not significantly different regarding their respective distances from QUALITY RELATIONSHIP.

The mateship attributes identified as crucial for African Americans are HONESTY, COMMUNICATION, LOVE, CARING, PATIENCE, TRUST, UNDERSTANDING, INTELLIGENT, RESPECT, PHYSICALLY ATTRACTIVE, SEXUALLY APPEALING, AFFECTION, and SUPPORT. The mean distances between QUALITY RELATIONSHIP and PERSONAL GROWTH IN RELATION TO (each attribute) are displayed in Table 8.4, arrayed such that those with the smallest distance (hence the most important variables) appear at the top of the list.

For a QUALITY RELATIONSHIP, PERSONAL GROWTH IN RELATION TO these attributes is important as follows, from most to least important, as indicated by mean distances from QUALITY RELATIONSHIP: RESPECT, COMMUNICATION, HONESTY, TRUST, CARING, LOVE, AFFECTION, UNDERSTANDING, SUPPORT, PATIENCE, INTELLIGENCE, PHYSICAL ATTRACTIVENESS, AND SEXUAL APPEAL. Z-scores of the differences among these personal growth variables reveal that PERSONAL GROWTH IN RELATION TO the last three on the list, which are also the traditional entry variables and entry variables for this sample, are significantly different from all the others.

Specifically, PERSONAL GROWTH IN RELATION TO SEXUAL APPEAL is significantly less important (p<.05) for relationship quality than

Table 8.4 Mean Distances Between QUALITY
RELATIONSHIP and PERSONAL GROWTH IN RELATION TO
Crucial Variables: African Americans

PERSONAL GROWTH IN RELATION TO...	MEAN DIST.
respect	15.73
communication	16.79
honesty	16.92
trust	17.10
caring	18.42
love	19.20
affection	20.68
understanding	20.70
support	21.23
patience	22.62
intelligence	38.97
physical attractiveness	52.82
sexual appeal	66.41

PERSONAL GROWTH IN RELATION TO: RESPECT ($z=3.19$), COMMUNICATION ($z=3.09$), HONESTY ($z=3.04$), TRUST ($z=3.11$), CARING ($z=2.61$), LOVE ($z=2.85$), AFFECTION ($z=2.29$), UNDERSTANDING ($z=2.44$), SUPPORT ($z=2.65$), and PATIENCE ($z=1.97$). PERSONAL GROWTH IN RELATION TO PHYSICAL ATTRACTIVENESS is significantly less important for relationship quality ($p<.05$) than PERSONAL GROWTH IN RELATION TO: RESPECT ($z=4.49$), COMMUNICATION ($z=4.38$), HONESTY ($z=4.31$), TRUST ($z=4.39$), CARING ($z=3.85$), LOVE ($z=4.06$), AFFECTION ($z=3.47$), UNDERSTANDING ($z=3.62$), SUPPORT ($z=3.81$), and PATIENCE ($z=3.10$). PERSONAL GROWTH IN RELATION TO INTELLIGENCE is significantly less important ($p<.05$) than PERSONAL GROWTH IN RELATION TO: RESPECT ($z=3.34$), COMMUNICATION ($z=3.23$), HONESTY ($z=3.18$), TRUST ($z=3.25$), CARING ($z=2.71$), LOVE ($z=2.96$), AFFECTION ($z=2.36$), UNDERSTANDING ($z=2.52$), SUPPORT ($z 2.74$), and PATIENCE ($z=2.02$). Finally, PERSONAL GROWTH IN RELATION TO INTELLIGENCE is significantly more important for relationship quality than PERSONAL GROWTH IN RELATION TO PHYSICAL ATTRACTIVENESS ($z=2.84$).

The mean distances between QUALITY RELATIONSHIP and GOOD COMMUNICATION ABOUT (each attribute) are displayed in Table 8.5, arrayed such that those with the smallest distance (hence the most important variables) appear at the top of the list. For a QUALITY RELATIONSHIP, GOOD COMMUNICATION ABOUT these attributes is important as follows, from most to least important, as indicated by mean distances from QUALITY RELATIONSHIP: TRUST, LOVE, AFFECTION, RESPECT, HONESTY, UNDERSTANDING, CARING, COMMUNICATION, SUPPORT, PATIENCE, INTELLIGENCE, PHYSICAL ATTRACTIVENESS, and SEXUAL APPEAL. There are several significant differences between these GOOD COMMUNICATION variables as regards their mean distance from QUALITY RELATIONSHIP—all of them again surrounding the traditional entry variables. GOOD COMMUNICATION ABOUT SEXUAL APPEAL, PHYSICAL ATTRACTIVENESS, and INTELLIGENCE are significantly ($p < .05$) less important for relationship quality than all the other GOOD COMMUNICATION variables.

Table 8.5 Mean Distances Between QUALITY RELATIONSHIP and GOOD COMMUNICATION ABOUT Crucial Variables: African Americans

GOOD COMMUNICATION ABOUT...	MEAN DIST.
trust	7.76
love	8.31
affection	8.63
respect	9.42
honesty	9.54
understanding	10.44
caring	11.62
communication	12.13
support	13.03
patience	14.72
intelligence	34.26
physical attractiveness	36.29
sexual appeal	46.95

Specifically, GOOD COMMUNICATION ABOUT SEXUAL APPEAL is significantly less important than TRUST ($z=3.43$), LOVE ($z=3.51$), AFFECTION ($z=2.47$), RESPECT ($z=2.80$), HONESTY ($z=3.35$), UNDERSTANDING ($z=2.75$), CARING ($z=2.88$), COMMUNICATION ($z=2.75$), SUPPORT ($z=2.57$), and PATIENCE ($z=2.14$). GOOD COMMUNICATION ABOUT PHYSICAL ATTRACTIVENESS is significantly less important than TRUST ($z=4.16$), LOVE ($z=4.24$), AFFECTION ($z=3.15$), RESPECT ($z=3.48$), HONESTY ($z=4.04$), UNDERSTANDING ($z=3.40$), CARING ($z=3.54$), COMMUNICATION ($z=3.37$), SUPPORT ($z=3.19$), and PATIENCE ($z=2.73$). GOOD COMMUNICATION ABOUT INTELLIGENCE is significantly less important than TRUST ($z=3.64$), LOVE ($z=3.72$), AFFECTION ($z=2.67$), RESPECT ($z=2.99$), HONESTY ($z=3.55$), UNDERSTANDING ($z=2.94$), CARING ($z=3.07$), COMMUNICATION ($z=2.93$), SUPPORT ($z=2.75$), and PATIENCE ($z=2.31$).

Table 8.6   Indicators of Relationship Quality:
African Amercians

QUALITY INDICATOR	% M	% F	% TOT
respect	50	100	83
love	50	100	83
understanding	50	38	42
trust	25	38	33
honesty	25	38	33
communication	25	25	25
mutual goals/values	25	25	25
commitment	25	25	25
support	0	38	25
listening	25	13	17
patience	25	13	17
understanding	25	13	17
unity	25	0	8
comfort w/ self	25	0	8
unconditional love	25	0	8
open mind	0	13	8
caring	0	13	8

Concerning RQ5, like the White American sample the relationship attributes generated for African Americans via the first research question seem to be representative of relational quality as well. In response to the open-ended question, only about two-thirds of the sample actually listed relationship quality indicators. The remaining third of the sample (two males and five females) simply referred to their original list of attributes (e.g., "see number 1"). The results from those who did list relationship quality indicators mirrors the list of relationship attributes. The results for this question are summarized in Table 8.6. Percentages in this table are computed based on the total number that actually filled in the item rather than referring to the attribute question.

Results and Interpretations: White Deaf Americans

The mean distance between QUALITY RELATIONSHIP and INTIMACY (GENERALLY) is 68.91; the mean distance between QUALITY RELATIONSHIP and INTIMACY (GENERALLY) is 63.48. A z-score of the difference between these two variables shows that they are not significantly different regarding their respective distances from QUALITY RELATIONSHIP.

The mateship attributes identified as crucial for Deaf White Americans of European descent are FUN, COMMUNICATION, HONESTY, LOVE, AFFECTION, SUPPORT, SEXUAL ATTRACTION, TRUST, (FRIENDSHIP), and RESPECT. The mean distances between QUALITY RELATIONSHIP and PERSONAL GROWTH IN RELATION TO (each attribute) are displayed in Table 8.7, arrayed such that those with the smallest distance (hence the most important variables) appear at the top of the list. For a QUALITY RELATIONSHIP, PERSONAL GROWTH IN RELATION to these attributes is important as follows, from most to least important, as indicated by mean distances from QUALITY RELATIONSHIP: TRUST, AFFECTION, SUPPORT, LOVE, HONESTY, RESPECT, COMMUNICATION, FUN, and SEXUAL ATTRACTION. Z-scores of the differences among these PERSONAL GROWTH variables reveal than none is significantly more important than any other for relationship quality.

The mean distances between QUALITY RELATIONSHIP and GOOD COMMUNICATION ABOUT (each attribute) are displayed in Table 8.8, arrayed such that those with the smallest distance (hence the most important variables) appear at the top of the list. For a QUALITY

Table 8.7 Mean Distances Between QUALITY
RELATIONSHIP and PERSONAL GROWTH IN RELATION TO
Crucial Variables: Deaf White Americans

PERSONAL GROWTH IN RELATION TO...	MEAN DIST.
trust	40.80
affection	41.20
support	42.20
love	42.80
honesty	45.28
respect	53.80
communication	54.48
fun	75.00
sexual attraction	85.40

Table 8.8 Mean Distances Between QUALITY
RELATIONSHIP and GOOD COMMUNICATION ABOUT
Crucial Variables: Deaf White Americans

GOOD COMMUNICATION ABOUT...	MEAN DIST.
trust	29.28
honesty	30.60
support	33.60
love	34.60
affection	35.00
respect	36.48
communication	37.64
fun	43.40
sexual attraction	65.48

RELATIONSHIP, GOOD COMMUNICATION ABOUT these attributes is important as follows, from most to least important, as indicated by mean distances from QUALITY RELATIONSHIP: TRUST, HONESTY, SUPPORT, LOVE, AFFECTION, RESPECT, COMMUNICATION, FUN, and SEXUAL

ATTRACTION. There are no significant differences between any of these GOOD COMMUNICATION variables as regards their mean distance from QUALITY RELATIONSHIP. All are of equal importance as shown by statistical tests.

Concerning RQ5, this cultural group also mirrored their list of attributes when considering relationship quality. In response to the open-ended question, participants did list several relationship quality indicators; again, the most frequently occurring on the list mirror the list of relationship attributes. In addition, about half the sample (two males and six females) referred to their original list of attributes. The results for this question are summarized in Table 8.9.

Results and Interpretation: Jamaica

The mean distance between QUALITY RELATIONSHIP and INTIMACY (GENERALLY) is 19.69; the mean distance between QUALITY RELATIONSHIP AND PERSONAL GROWTH (GENERALLY) is 25.27. A z-score of the difference between these two variables shows that they are not significantly different regarding their respective distances from QUALITY RELATIONSHIP.

The mateship attributes identified as crucial for Jamaicans are TRUST, LOVE, HONESTY, RESPECT, COMMUNICATION, UNDERSTANDING, CARING, (FRIENDSHIP), AFFECTION, SHARING, SUPPORT, PHYSICALLY ATTRACTIVE, INTELLIGENCE, and SEXUALLY APPEALING. The mean distances between QUALITY RELATIONSHIP and PERSONAL GROWTH IN RELATION TO (each attribute) are displayed in Table 8.10, arrayed such that those with the smallest distance (hence the most important variables) appear at the top of the list.

For a QUALITY RELATIONSHIP, PERSONAL GROWTH IN RELATION TO these attributes is important as follows, from most to least important, as indicated by mean distances from QUALITY RELATIONSHIP: RESPECT, HONESTY, COMMUNICATION, TRUST, UNDERSTANDING, LOVE, CARING, AFFECTION, SHARING, SUPPORT, SEX APPEAL, PHYSICAL ATTRACTIVENESS, and INTELLIGENCE. Z-scores of the differences among these personal growth variables reveal only one significant (p<.05) difference. PERSONAL GROWTH IN RELATION TO HONESTY is significantly closer to QUALITY RELATIONSHIP than is PERSONAL GROWTH IN RELATION TO PHYSICAL ATTRACTIVENESS (z=1.99).

Table 8.9 Indicators of Relationship Quality:
Deaf White Americans

QUALITY INDICATOR	% M	% F	% TOT
communication	50	67	68
trust	25	40	47
honesty	25	27	37
respect	0	40	32
doing what you want	25	7	21
commitment	25	0	16
faithful	25	0	16
pursue despite odds	25	0	16
love	0	13	11
sharing	0	13	11
accept. of personal ideas	0	7	5
affection	0	7	5
being there	0	7	5
clear objectives	0	7	5
compatible	0	7	5
dedication	0	7	5
each need own space	0	7	5
empathy	0	7	5
friendship	0	7	5
listen	0	7	5
patience	0	7	5
sex	0	7	5
sincerirty	0	7	5
supporting	0	7	5
understanding	0	7	5

The mean distances between QUALITY RELATIONSHIP, GOOD COMMUNICATION ABOUT (each attribute) are displayed in Table 8.11, arrayed such that those with the smallest distance (hence the most important variables) appear at the top of the list. For a QUALITY RELATIONSHIP, GOOD COMMUNICATION ABOUT these attributes is important as follows, from most to least important, as indicated by mean distances from QUALITY RELATIONSHIP: RESPECT, COMMUNICATION, CARING, UNDERSTANDING, HONESTY, LOVE, AFFECTION, SUPPORT, SHARING, SEX APPEAL, TRUST, INTELLIGENCE, and PHYSICAL

Table 8.10   Mean Distances Between QUALITY RELATIONSHIP and PERSONAL GROWTH IN RELATION TO Crucial Variables: Jamaicans

PERSONAL GROWTH IN RELATION TO...	MEAN DIST.
respect	16.71
honesty	19.08
communication	19.46
trust	20.02
understanding	20.10
love	20.63
caring	22.88
affection	25.10
sharing	25.79
support	29.52
sex appeal	31.15
physically attractive	34.50
intelligence	54.60

ATTRACTIVENESS. One significant difference (p < .05) occurs. GOOD COMMUNICATION ABOUT HONESTY is significantly more important than GOOD COMMUNICATION ABOUT PHYSICAL ATTRACTIVENESS.

Concerning RQ5, the relationship attributes generated for the first research question seem to be representative of relational quality as well. In response to the open-ended question, participants

Table 8.11 Mean Distances Between QUALITY
RELATIONSHIP and GOOD COMMUNICATION ABOUT
Crucial Variables: Jamaicans

GOOD COMMUNICATION ABOUT...	MEAN DIST.
respect	19.18
communication	19.35
caring	20.12
understanding	20.44
honesty	20.80
love	20.82
affection	21.00
support	22.64
sharing	23.44
sex appeal	25.08
trust	26.67
intelligence	28.32
physically attractive	32.80

listed several relationship quality indicators, but the most frequently occurring on the list mirror the list of relationship attributes. In addition, five respondents (one male and four females) also
directly referred to their original list of attributes. The results for
this question are summarized in Table 8.12.

Conclusions

As in the analyses in Chapter Seven, only open-ended responses will be discussed for the Deaf White American sample because of
the inconclusive nature of the Galileo data. Intracultural comparisons of the ways in which attributes operate as maintenance and
quality variables is quite interesting. For European Americans,
several of the attributes are ranked similarly as maintenance variables, personal growth quality variables, and good communication
quality variables. Love and trust rank high; support ranks low;

Table 8.12   Indicators of Relationship Quality: Jamaicans

QUALITY INDICATOR	% M	% F	% TOT	QUALITY INDICATOR	% M	% F	% TOT
love	40	67	55	sex	20	0	9
trust	60	50	55	be there	0	8	5
communciation	20	50	36	be with	0	8	5
honesty	20	42	32	gentleness	0	8	5
respect	20	42	32	individuality	0	8	5
understanding	20	42	32	kindness	0	8	5
caring	0	25	14	meekness	0	8	5
faithfulness	0	25	14	self control	0	8	5
acceptance	20	8	14	sincerity	0	8	5
commitment	20	8	14	appreciation	10	0	5
giving	20	8	14	common interests	10	0	5
compatibility	0	17	9	devotion	10	0	5
compromise	0	17	9	discuss anything	10	0	5
consideration	0	17	9	honor	10	0	5
friendship/best	0	17	9	hope to continue	10	0	5
humor	0	17	9	money	10	0	5
open	0	17	9	quality partner	10	0	5
patience	0	17	9	relationship progress	10	0	5
sharing	0	17	9	showing interest	10	0	5
stability	0	17	9	similar morals	10	0	5
religion	20	0	9	working on relationship	10	0	5

sexual appeal, physical attractiveness, and intelligence rank lowest. Communication is the only attribute ranked dissimilarly across the three categories: in the middle as a maintenance variable and low as a good communication quality variable, but first as a personal growth quality variable. In comparison, love ranks first as a maintenance variable, and caring ranks first as a good communication quality variable. Three attributes are ranked similarly as maintenance and good communication quality variables. Caring ranks high; honesty and respect rank in the middle. Finally, loyalty and affection rank similarly as maintenance and personal growth quality variables—the former in the mid to high range but low as a good communication quality variable, and the latter in the mid to low range but high as a good communication quality variable. (See tables 7.1, 8.1, and 8.2.)

For African Americans, several of the attributes are also ranked similarly as maintenance variables, personal growth quality variables, and good communication quality variables. Trust ranks high—first as both a maintenance and a good communication quality variable and more toward the middle as a personal growth quality variable. Love also ranks high—first as a personal growth quality variable, second as a maintenance variable, and more toward the middle as a good communication quality variable. Other attributes that rank similarly across the three categories include honesty (mid to high), caring (mid), and patience, support, sexual appeal, physical attractiveness, and intelligence (all low). Understanding ranks highly as a maintenance variable, but in the mid range as a good communication quality variable and in the low to mid range as a personal growth quality variable. Love ranks high as a good communication quality variable, but in the mid range as a maintenance variable and a personal growth quality variable. Finally, two variables are dissimilar across the three categories. Communication ranks highly as a personal growth quality variable, in the mid range as a maintenance variable, and low as a good communication quality variable. Affection ranks highly as a good communication quality variable, in the mid range as a personal growth quality variable, and low as a maintenance variable. (See tables 7.6, 8.4, and 8.5.)

For Jamaicans, most of the attributes are ranked similarly across the three categories. Honesty, respect, and understanding rank fairly high across all three categories; love ranks in the middle range; sharing ranks mid-to-low; physical attractiveness, support, intelligence, and sex appeal rank low.

However, there are some interesting differences. Trust ranks high as both a maintenance and a personal growth quality variable but low as a good communication quality variable. Affection ranks high as a maintenance variable, but in the low middle range as a personal growth quality variable and in middle range as a good communication quality variable. Communication ranks high for both quality categories, but in the mid-to-low range for maintenance. Caring differs across all three categories (low for maintenance, middle-range for personal growth, and high for good communication). (See Tables 7.16, 8.10, and 8.11). All three cultures seem to have a high degree of intracultural homogeneity across the three categories.

An intercultural comparison of three cultures (European Americans, African Americans, and Jamaicans) for relational quality is quite interesting. For relational quality the two American co-cultures have distinctly different patterns. One of the important differences lies in the different levels of importance placed on personal growth in relation to respect. For African Americans, personal growth on respect is most closely related to relational quality. However, for European Americans personal growth in relation to respect is far down the list, in ninth place. The two groups are similar in the importance they place on personal growth in relation to communication, honesty, trust, love, caring, affection, support, sexual appeal, intelligence, and physical attractiveness. Obviously, personal growth in relation to respect is as important for relational quality as it is for relational maintenance to this African American sample, and this European American sample does not seem to share this value (see Chapter Seven).

As a "good communication" variable, respect does not carry the same primary importance for African Americans. Apparently, this is not an attribute that needs to be talked about to be manifested as a personal growth quality variable. For good communication about the attributes, African Americans place a higher value than European Americans on trust (ranked first and fourth, respectively). Conversely, European Americans place more importance on caring (ranked first and seventh, respectively). The rankings of the rest of the attributes are almost identical, although respect is slightly higher for African Americans (fourth, as compared to sixth). A comparison of Tables 8.1, 8.2, 8.4, and 8.5 is quite revealing. Although these findings show that the two cultures are quite similar in the crucial attributes themselves (to be discussed in Chapter Nine), the importance of these attributes for relational quality differs in few, but important ways. Like the results for relational maintenance, these few differences have important implications for interracial relationships (to be discussed in Chapter Nine).

These studies show that the two American co-cultures are also quite similar to Jamaican culture, particularly for personal growth quality variables. The three groups place similar levels of importance on personal growth in relation to the following: honesty, communication, trust, love, caring, affection, sex appeal, physical attractiveness, and intelligence. The differences for understanding and support are slight; Jamaicans see understanding as more important than do African Americans (fifth and eighth, respectively) and rank support somewhat lower than European Americans (tenth and seventh, respectively). Like African Americans, Jamaicans rank personal growth in relation to respect as the most important quality variable; for European Americans it ranks eighth.

The differences for good communication quality variables between Jamaican culture and the two American co-cultures are more striking. Respect is first for Jamaicans, but sixth for European Americans and fourth for African Americans. Communication is second for Jamaicans, but low for the two American groups (ninth and eighth). Caring is third for Jamaicans; this is similar to European Americans (first) but not for African Americans (seventh). Love, affection, and trust—which all rank highly for the two American groups—are low on the Jamaican list (sixth, seventh, and eleventh, respectively). The remaining good communication variables are quite similar among the three groups.

It is also quite interesting to compare the cultures on their lists of relational quality indicators. Like their lists of conflict sources, all groups generated quite similar and rather predictable indicators of relational quality—lists that are quite similar to their basic relationship attributes (see Tables 8.3, 8.6, 8.9, and 8.12).

The European American sample generated the longest overall list, probably due to the fact that there were more respondents who answered the question and hence the possibility of more unique (mentioned by only one person) quality indicators. There appears to be less intracultural homogeneity for European Americans on relational quality indicators than for conflict sources. The same pattern occurs for Deaf European Americans and for Jamaicans—although the Deaf list was quite a bit shorter, probably because of the language factor discussed previously. Conversely, the African American sample appears to be more homogeneous for quality indicators than for conflict sources (see Chapter Seven).

Future research is needed to examine cross-cultural differences in meaning for these terms. In addition, much work is yet to be done in analyzing how these findings contribute to the broad literature on relational quality.

CHAPTER NINE

CONCLUSIONS, INTERPRETATIONS, AND SPECULATIONS

Introduction

In their concluding chapter, Nicotera and Associates (1993) draw several conclusions regarding their work on Cushman and Associates' general theory. First, an individual will be interpersonally attracted to those whom s/he perceives to provide him/her with self-concept support. Second, different types of relationships are based on different types of perceived self-concept support. Third, interpersonal relationships progress through discrete, identifiable levels of intimacy; further, entry into such relationships depends on the communication of self-concept support on a set of crucial variables, and relational progression is dependent on the communication of self-concept support on another set of crucial variables. These conclusions correspond to Propositions 1 through 3 (see Table 1.1).

Their recommendations for future research are three-fold: first, thorough testing of the seven propositions—1–4 in other cultural settings and 5–7 in general; second, dyadic longitudinal investigation; and third, investigations of actual interaction to fully assess the role of communication in the relationship formation and development process. They also argue for expanding the theory's scope. The process of explicating the propositions is a necessary foundation to longitudinal dyadic study, analysis of interaction, and theoretic expansion. Hence, this present volume has presented several studies that accomplish the location of levels and attributes in several American co-cultures and in two non-American

139

cultures—one Western and one Eastern. Further, the studies begin the process of testing Propositions 5 and 7 in the Western cultures. It was considered premature to launch a study of Proposition 6 until 5 had been investigated more fully. This volume, therefore, represents applications to several cultures of the general theory (as summarized by the propositions). This has resulted in an unavoidable redundancy in the organization and presentation of studies in several of the chapters.

A Multicultural View

The applications of the general theory presented in this volume provide credence to Ju's (in Nicotera and Associates 1993) framework of mateship as cultural choice. Following Chu (1979, 1985), he argues that culture consists of three major components in the life of the self: First, the social relations with significant others; second, objects in the physical environment that mediate social relations; and third, ideas (ideology, values, beliefs) that influence perception of and set priorities for the first two components. Mate relationships are a part of the first component. In Ju's words, "mate selection is by nature a cultural action" (Nicotera and Associates 1993, 202).

Following the logic of a cultural-choice framework...mate relationships are seen as dependent on two crucial sets of variables—both of which arise from cultural imperatives. These variables are, of course, entry and intensity variables. The theoretic structure is multicultural since it predicts the general pattern of relationship initiation and growth, yet does not dictate the specific character of the crucial variables. First, before a dyad can enter into a...mate relationship, they must perceive each other as having the basic attributes of a...mate (dictated by the culture) and must provide self-concept support to each other on those variables. Second, for the relationship to deepen, they must perceive each other as having increasingly intense levels of a set of key attributes (dictated by the culture) and must provide self-concept support to each other on those variables. (Nicotera and Associates 1993, 220)

It must also be noted that however multiculturally applicable, the conceptualization and operationalization of these constructs are achieved through the decidedly Western theoretic tradition of the rules perspective. Ju (in Nicotera and Associates 1993) applauds the theory of relationships developed in that volume and tested in this one for its ability to transcend the Western-imposed values that limit other theories of interpersonal relations. However, the theory espoused herein is undoubtedly a Western theory in its modes of inquiry, interpretation, and explanation. As Ju (in Nicotera and Associates 1993) notes, the theory is applicable to non-Western cultures without imposing Western values on the process of interpersonal relations. However, the research endeavor itself relies on Western ideals of inquiry, interpretation, and explanation.

Cultural Comparisons

According to these studies, the following mateship attributes for European Americans have high intracultural homogeneity: trust, friendship, love, honesty, communication, caring, and loyalty. Physical attractiveness, sexual attraction, intelligence, respect, support, and affection have a lower degree of intracultural homogeneity. For African Americans, honesty, communication, love, caring, patience, trust, and understanding have high intracultural homogeneity; intelligence, respect, physical attractiveness, sexual appeal, affection, and support have less intracultural homogeneity. For Deaf European Americans the intraculturally homogeneous attributes are fun, communication, honesty, love, affection, support, sexual attraction, trust, and friendship; respect has lower homogeneity.

These lists are quite similar, but distinct differences exist among them. For the African American sample, patience and understanding are crucial attributes, but they do not appear on either of the European American lists. Conversely, friendship and loyalty, crucial attributes for the hearing European American sample, are not on the African American list; loyalty also does not appear on the White Deaf list. The White Deaf list suggests quite compellingly that Deaf Culture has a distinct mateship pattern;

intelligence and physical attractiveness were not even mentioned. Caring was mentioned but did not make the thirty percent criterion, and respect was extremely low on the list below that criterion. Fun, first on the list, was unique to this cultural sample.

Whereas many of the attributes for these three American co-cultures are the same, the order of their importance differs. Tables 2.1, 3.1, and 4.1 display the order of importance. For the African American sample, honesty is the most important attribute; for the hearing European American sample, trust is the most important; and for the Deaf European American sample, fun is most important. These attributes also operate differently for the hearing European American sample and the African American sample. The most important differences are that for the African American sample, intelligence is an entry variable and respect an intensity variable. The pattern is the opposite for the hearing European American sample. Because of the difficulty with the Galileo data for Deaf Culture, no conclusions can be drawn about the nature of attributes as entry or intensity variables.

The semantic labels for mateship levels also have important differences for these U.S. samples. The hearing European American sample makes a significant distinction between occasional date and exclusive date; whereas the African American sample does not make a distinction between levels of dating. In addition, "engaged" was clearly a more salient level of the mate relationship in the African American data. Again, because of the difficulty with the Deaf Culture Galileo data, conclusions cannot be drawn about the statistical significance of the mateship levels. However, like their hearing counterparts, the Deaf European American sample does make a qualitative distinction between a casual and a steady stage of dating; further, similar to the African American sample, an engagement stage seemed to be salient for this group.

Attributes in the Jamaican data were quite similar to the American data: trust, love, honesty, respect, communication, understanding, caring, friendship, affection, sharing, and to a lesser extent, physical attractiveness, support, intelligence, and sexual appeal. Important comparisons to the American samples include, first, that respect and affection made the thirty percent criterion, revealing that these traditionally assumed American mateship attributes are more salient for the Jamaican sample than for any of the American samples. Second, the Jamaican data is similar to the African American data in that understanding is a crucial attribute, but also similar to both Deaf and hearing European American data in that friendship is a crucial attribute. Like the European American sample, trust is the most important attribute for the Jamaican sample. In addition, communication ranks lower for the Jamaicans and European Americans than for the African Americans and Deaf European Americans. Finally, the Jamaican sample lists caring as a crucial attribute; this variable is unique to this culture.

The semantic labels for mateship levels also have important differences between the Jamaican and U.S. samples. Like the data from African American culture the data from Jamaican culture do not reveal a distinction between pre-committed levels of dating. However, the concepts of engagement and marriage seem to operate quite differently in Jamaica than in either U.S. co-culture. These formal institutional practices simply do not seem to be indicators of relational stages for the Jamaicans sampled. It may be that the formal institutionalization of personal relationships is a practice with much more relational meaning in the United States than in Jamaica.

Although the nature of the Deaf Culture Galileo data precludes meaningful comparisons between this U.S. co-culture and Jamaican culture, we may cautiously conclude that the Deaf European Americans sampled are more similar to their hearing counterparts than to either cultural group of African descent in that they do make a qualitative distinction between a casual and a steady stage of dating. In addition, they are more similar to African Americans than to Jamaicans in that an engagement stage seemed salient. Finally, like the other U.S. co-cultures, Deaf European Americans differ from Jamaicans in the importance placed on formalization of the mate relationship.

As expected, results for Japanese culture were distinctly different from those of all the other cultures studied. For male respondents, the crucial attributes are beautiful, good cook, kind, youth, love, and honest; for females they are love, wealthy, fun, honest, sportsman, employed, kind, and happy. (An intracultural comparison of males and females appears in Chapter Six.) Kindness is unique to this sample as a crucial mateship attribute, regardless of gender. The Japanese male respondents differ from any other group surveyed in the importance they place on having a physically attractive, domestically skilled, and youthful mate. Conversely, the Japanese female respondents differ from any other group surveyed by placing primary importance on love and on having an athletic, employed, and happy mate. The Japanese female and Deaf European American samples are alike in the importance they place on fun in a mate relationship. Finally, the results suggest that love and honesty are crucial mateship attributes for all the cultures studied. Although it increases at different junctures for each culture, love is a growth-related variable. Honesty is an intensity variable for U.S. co-cultures and Jamaicans, but an entry variable in Japan.

Implications for Intercultural Relationships

Earlier work in this tradition (see Nicotera and Associates 1993) notes the implications of intercultural diversity for the initiation and growth of intercultural mate relationships, which correspond to Propositions 1–4 (see Table 1.1).

Diversity between cultures concerning the attributes necessary for mateship formation and growth complicate the development of intercultural mateship....The greater the diversity between cultures, the more difficult intercultural mateship development would be. In the attempt to initiate and/or develop a mate relationship, two individuals of diverse cultures provide communication of support on different sets of attributes....For intercultural mateship to develop, each individual must be sensitive to the different expectations of the other for entry into and growth of such relationships. (Nicotera and Associates 1993, 190-191)

The investigations into conflict, relational maintenance (Chapter Seven), and quality (Chapter Eight) allow us to expand this discussion to Propositions 5 and 7. Following are several speculations surrounding the propositions as they are applied to specific intercultural pairings. Again, these are speculations; the data do not warrant drawing conclusions on intercultural relationships, especially due to their self-report format. These speculations seem to support the research findings that commitment and satisfaction patterns and their expectations differ racially (Davis and Strube 1993) and that intercultural mateships are less stable than intracultural pairings (Lewis, Robinson and Yancy 1995).

African American/European American mateship pairs. According to these data, African American and European American expectations for mate relationships are similar. However, there are crucial differences that may have implications for the success of such relationships. For both samples, physical attractiveness is an entry variable. However, for the African American sample, intelligence and sexual appeal are entry variables whereas for the European Americans intelligence is an intensity variable and sexual appeal is a marker variable (significantly increasing at the point of clearing the field). Because the crucial attributes are so similar, these results predict that the initiation of a mate-type relationship between a black/white pair is likely to be simple. The only barricade to initiation of the relationship suggested by these data is that the white partner may expect to feel s/he is in a friendship before entering into a mate relationship. These studies suggest the white partner's field of approachables is more constrained. According to these data, a European American will not attempt to initiate a mate-type relationship in the absence of a feeling of friendship. These studies suggest that attempts by an African American individual to initiate a mate-type relationship with a European American individual will likely be rejected if the European American individual does not perceive a feeling of friendship. Beyond this difference, the results suggest that both individuals must manifest self-concept support for the other's physical attractiveness, sexual appeal, intelligence, and respect.

The results imply that growth of the relationship might be more complicated. Although neither partner is likely to expect self-concept support of physical attractiveness to increase, the European American partner may expect an increase in self-concept support of sexual appeal before the relationship can progress to "clearing the field." The data suggest that the European American partner may also expect self-concept support of intelligence to increase, neither of which the African American partner probably expects to increase. Further, we may predict the African American partner—but not the European American partner—to expect self-concept support of respect to increase.

To further complicate matters, the results suggest that the African American partner will attempt to provide and will expect to receive self-concept support to be communicated on patience and understanding—both of which the European American partner will not provide and will not expect to receive. Conversely, the European American partner may attempt to provide and may expect self-concept support to be communicated on friendship and loyalty (the latter of which must increase for the field to be cleared)—both of which the African American partner is unlikely to provide or expect to receive. Other differences are more subtle. The data lead to the speculation that the African American partner will expect a constant increase in love and communication; whereas the European American partner expects an increase in love only at the point when a formal public declaration of marriage is made and expects an increase in communication only at the point when the field is cleared. Overall, for this relationship to deepen and grow, each partner must be sensitive to the needs and expectations of the other. Further, each must be able to articulate his/her needs and expectations for self-concept support. Such simple and personal expectations for self-concept support must be communicated and positively responded to for an interracial couple to develop the strength to withstand the great societal obstacles they will certainly face in the United States' racially divided society.

The results lead us to expect that the partners will also differ in their expectations for what allows them to maintain their relationship. For the European American sample, the maintenance of self-concept support on love is most important, with trust a close second. For the African American sample, however, self-concept support on love is well down the list. Self-concept support on trust, respect, understanding, honesty, communication, and caring are all more important than love. The European Americans placed respect at a much lower level of importance for relational maintenance. The implications of these differences (see Tables 7.1 and 7.6) are that once an interracial pair is able to build an intimate relationship, they must be vigilant to the differences between them regarding expectations for maintaining that intimacy. Again, each must be sensitive to the other's needs and willing to communicate her/his own needs.

When this couple faces conflict, results suggest it is likely to be about jealousy, other friends, time together, and money. The European American partner may expect that conflict will increase as the relationship deepens (except for conflict about other friends, which s/he expects to remain the same). The African American partner may expect that conflict about all of these things will decrease as the relationship deepens. The implication of these results is clear; the African American partner is likely to be faced with unexpected conflict about these issues. On the other hand, the open-ended data (see Tables 7.5 and 7.10) show that the African Americans, at all levels of relationship, perceive more potential sources of conflict than do the European Americans. It is unclear whether the African American cultural tendency to directly confront and honestly deal with conflict (Kochman 1982; Martin, Hecht, and Larkey 1994) would compensate for these differing patterns.

Finally, once the pair has surmounted their cultural differences to initiate, develop, and maintain a mate relationship, these results show that their perceptions about the quality of their relationship are likely to be different. According to these data, the African American partner may perceive the highest quality relationship to be one which fosters personal growth in relation to respect and facilitates good communication about trust. Conversely, the European American partner may not perceive personal growth in relation to respect as a primary indicator of relational quality, and may perceive the highest quality relationship to be one which facilitates good communication about caring.

Hearing and Deaf American mateship pairs. According to these studies, hearing and Deaf European American expectations for mate relationships are also similar. We might predict that both partners in such a relationship would expect to provide and receive self-concept support for trust, friendship, love, honesty, communication, affection, respect, support, and sexual appeal. Further, we might predict that the hearing partner would also expect to provide and receive self-concept support for caring, loyalty, physical attractiveness, and intelligence—which the Deaf partner may not expect to provide or receive. Finally, we might predict that the Deaf partner would expect to provide and receive self-concept support for fun—which the hearing partner would not expect to provide or receive. The results of these studies suggest that a hearing African American/Deaf European American pair would have differences as well. According to the data, both would expect to provide and receive self-concept support for honesty, communication, love, trust, respect, sexual appeal, affection, and support. However, the Deaf European American partner may also expect to provide and receive self-concept support for fun—which the hearing partner would not expect to provide. The hearing African American partner may also expect to provide and receive self-concept support for caring, patience, understanding, intelligence, and physical attractiveness—which the Deaf partner may not expect to provide or receive. Because of the invalid nature of the Galileo data for Deaf Culture, speculations of implications for entry and intensity variables, maintenance, and quality cannot be attempted.

European American/Jamaican mateship pairs. Patterns in the data for European American and Jamaican expectations for mate relationships are similar. For both samples, physical attractiveness is an entry variable; both partners may expect to provide and receive a constant level of self-concept support for physical attractiveness. Trust, honesty, caring, affection, and support are intensity variables; both partners may expect self-concept support to increase on these attributes. However, as with other intercultural pairings, there are crucial differences between these samples that may have implications for the success of such relationships. For the Jamaican sample, intelligence is an entry variable whereas for European Americans intelligence is an intensity variable; sexual appeal is an intensity variable for Jamaicans but a marker variables for European Americans; and friendship is an intensity variable for Jamaicans but an entry variable for European Americans. The data suggest that the Jamaican partner may expect to provide and receive constant self-concept support for intelligence and increasing self-concept support for sexual appeal, friendship, and respect; whereas the European American may expect to provide and receive increasing self support for intelligence, increasing self-concept support for sexual appeal only until the field is cleared, and a constant level of self-concept support for friendship and respect.

The Jamaican partner may also expect love to constantly increase; whereas the European American partner may only expect an increase at the point of commitment. Similarly, the Jamaican partner may expect communication to steadily increase, but the European American partner may expect the increase to level off once the field has been cleared. To further complicate matters, the data suggest that the Jamaican partner may attempt to provide and may expect increasing self-concept support to be communicated on understanding and sharing—both of which the European American partner may neither provide nor expect. Conversely, the European American partner may attempt to provide and may expect self-concept support to be communicated on loyalty (which must increase for the field to be cleared)—which the Jamaican partner may neither provide nor expect. Finally, the difference between the two cultures regarding the importance of formalizing the relationship may indicate a problem for such couples.

The patterns in the data also suggest that the partners may differ in their expectations for what allows them to maintain their relationship. For the European American sample, the maintenance of self-concept support on love is most important, with trust a close second. For the Jamaican sample, however, self-concept support on love is farther down the list. Self-concept support on affection, trust, honesty, and respect are all more important than love. The European American sample places affection and respect at a much lower level of importance and caring at a much higher level of importance for relational maintenance. The implications of these differences (see Tables 7.1 and 7.16) are that once a pair is able to build an intimate relationship, they must be vigilant to the differences between them regarding expectations for maintaining that intimacy. Again, each must be sensitive to the other's needs and willing to communicate her/his own needs.

When this couple faces conflict, it is likely to be about jealousy. Both samples seem to expect that such conflict will increase as the relationship deepens. The European American partner may be faced with unexpected conflict about insecurity and communication; the Jamaican with unexpected conflict about other friends, time together, and money.

Finally, once the pair has surmounted their cultural differences to initiate, develop, and maintain a mate relationship, their perceptions about the quality of their relationship are likely to be slightly different. The Jamaican partner may expect personal growth in relation to respect to be a primary indicator of quality, whereas the European American partner may not. The Jamaican partner may perceive good communication about respect and communication to be important indicators of quality; whereas the European American partner may perceive good communication about love, affection, and trust to indicate quality.

African American/Jamaican mateship pairs. African American and Jamaican expectations for mate relationships are much more similar in these studies. Physical attractiveness and intelligence are entry variables; both partners may expect to provide and receive steady levels of self-concept support on these attributes. Trust, love, honesty, respect, communication, understanding, caring, affection, and support are intensity variables for both samples; both partners may expect to provide and receive increasing amounts of self-concept support on these attributes. However, as with other intercultural pairings, there are crucial differences that have implications for the success of such relationships. Sexual appeal is an intensity variable for the Jamaican sample but an entry variable for the African Americans. The Jamaican partner may expect self-concept support on this attribute to steadily increase; whereas the African American partner may expect the level of self-concept support to remain stable. Furthermore, the Jamaican partner may expect to provide and receive increasing self-concept support for friendship and sharing, neither of which his/her African American partner may expect to receive or provide. Conversely, the African American partner may expect to provide and receive increasing self-concept support for patience, which the Jamaican may not expect at all. Finally, like European Americans, African Americans seem to place a higher value on the formal institutionalization of the relationship than do Jamaicans.

The partners may also differ in their expectations for what allows them to maintain their relationship. For the Jamaican sample, the maintenance of self-concept support on affection is most important, with trust a close second. For African American respondents, however, self-concept support on affection is well down the list. Self-concept support on trust, respect, understanding, honesty, communication, caring, love, patience, and support are all more important than love. The African American sample also places understanding at a much higher level of importance than the Jamaican respondents. The implications of these differences (see Tables 7.6 and 7.16) are that once the pair is able to build an intimate relationship, they must be vigilant to the differences between them regarding expectations for maintaining that intimacy. Again, each must be sensitive to the other's needs and willing to communicate her/his own needs.

When this couple faces conflict, it is likely to be about jealousy. The African American respondents expect that such conflict will decrease as the relationship deepens. The Jamaicans expect that such conflict will increase. The implication is clear; the African American partner may be faced with unexpected conflict about jealousy at later stages of the relationship and with unexpected conflict about insecurity and communication at all stages. The Jamaican partner may be faced with unexpected conflict about other friends, money, and time together.

Finally, once the pair has surmounted their cultural differences to initiate, develop, and maintain a mate relationship, their perceptions about the quality of their relationship are likely to be different. The African American sample perceives the highest quality relationship to be one that fosters personal growth in relation to respect and facilitates good communication about trust. Although the Jamaican sample also perceives personal growth in relation to respect as a primary indicator of relational quality, they perceive the highest quality relationship to be one that facilitates good communication about respect as well. Good communication about trust is not an important indicator of quality for the Jamaicans.

European American/Japanese mateship pairs. European American and Japanese expectations for mate relationships are quite different in these studies. Because Japanese males and females have such different expectations for providing and receiving self-concept support, we will first consider the pairing of a European American female with a Japanese male. For both of these samples, physical attractiveness is an entry variable. She may expect to both provide and receive self-concept support on this variable; he may only expect to provide it. For the female European American sample, friendship and respect are also entry variables on which they expect to both provide and receive self-concept support—neither of which the Japanese males expect to provide or receive. The male Japanese sample expects to provide self-concept support for the partner's cooking ability, kindness, youth, and honesty as entry variables and expects to receive self-concept support for their own wealth, fun, honesty, sportsmanship, kindness, and happiness—none of which they expect to provide or receive (except honesty). Honesty would not be expected to present a problem at the initiation stage of the relationship, since it is also a crucial attribute for the European Americans. Because the crucial attributes are so dissimilar, initiation of a mate-type relationship between a European American female and a Japanese male may be expected to be quite difficult.

If such a relationship is successfully initiated, the growth of the relationship may be quite complicated. Although neither partner may expect self-concept support of physical attractiveness to increase, the female European American partner may expect to provide and receive a continuation of self-concept support for friendship and respect. She may expect to provide and receive increasing self-concept support of communication, loyalty, and sexual appeal before the relationship can progress to "clearing the field;" she may also expect to provide and receive increasing self-concept support of trust, caring, intelligence, support, and affection—none of which the Japanese male partner may expect to provide or receive at all. The Japanese male may expect to provide a constant level of self-concept support for his partner's cooking ability, kindness, and youth—none of which she may expect or need—and to receive a constant level of self-concept support for his own wealth, fun, sportsmanship, kindness, and happiness—none of which she may expect to provide. To even further complicate matters, the female European American partner may expect love to increase only at the point when a public declaration of marriage is made; whereas her Japanese male partner may expect love to increase only at the point when the field is cleared. Finally, the Japanese male partner may expect only to both provide and receive self-concept support for honesty at a constant level; whereas his female European American partner may expect to provide and receive increasing self-concept support for honesty.

These studies show that male European American and female Japanese expectations have almost no similarities. However, because their dissimilarities are so complete, they may be better able to develop sensitivity to them. Historically, this gender composition of this intercultural pairing has been more common—a fact that may be largely attributed to existing fields of availables stemming from U.S. servicemen in Japan. However, as history has progressed, the field of availables has increased for the opposite gender pairing without a concomitant increase in the occurrence of these relationships. The complete dissimilarity of expectation between European American men and Japanese women shown in these studies may indeed increase the partners' sensitivity to differences. This would offer a plausible explanation as to why this gender composition of this intercultural pairing continues to be more common.

For both of these samples, physical attractiveness is an entry variable. He may expect to both provide and receive self-concept support on this variable; she may only expect to receive it. For the male European American partner, friendship and respect are also entry variables on which he may expect to both provide and receive self-concept support—neither of which she may expect to provide or receive. In addition, the female Japanese partner may expect to provide self-concept support for her partner's wealth, fun, honesty, sportsmanship, kindness, and happiness and may expect to receive self-concept support for her own cooking ability, kindness, youth, and honesty—none of which he may expect to provide or receive (except honesty). Again, honesty would not seem to present a problem at the initiation stage of the relationship, since it is also a crucial attribute for the European American sample.

If such a relationship is successfully initiated, the growth of the relationship may be quite complicated. Although neither partner may expect his self-concept support of her physical attractiveness to increase, the male European American partner may expect to receive a continuation of self-concept support for physical attractiveness (which she may not expect to provide), and he may expect to both provide and receive a continuation of self-concept support for friendship and respect—neither of which she may expect to provide or receive. He may expect to provide and receive increasing self-concept support of communication, loyalty, and sexual appeal before the relationship can progress to "clearing the field;" he may also expect to provide and receive increasing self-concept support of trust, caring, intelligence, support, and affection to increase—none of which the Japanese female partner may expect to provide or receive at all. The Japanese female may expect to provide a constant level of self-concept support for her partner's wealth, fun, sportsmanship, kindness, and happiness and to receive a constant level of self-concept support for her own cooking ability, kindness, and youth—none of which he may expect to receive or to provide, respectively. To even further complicate matters, the male European American partner may expect love to increase only at the point when a public declaration of marriage is made; whereas his Japanese female partner may expect love to increase only at the point when the field is cleared. The Japanese female partner may expect only to both provide and receive self-concept support for honesty at a constant level; whereas her male European American partner may expect to provide and receive increasing self-concept support for honesty. Finally, the Japanese female may expect to increase her self-concept support for his employment at the point when a public declaration of engagement is made.

African American/Japanese mateship pairs. The African American and Japanese samples' expectations for mate relationships are also quite different. Again, because Japanese males and females have such different expectations for providing and receiving self-concept support, we will first consider the pairing of an African American female with a Japanese male. For both of these samples, physical attractiveness is an entry variable. She may expect to both provide and receive self-concept support on this variable; he may only expect to provide it. For the female African American, sexual appeal and intelligence are also entry variables on which she may expect to both provide and receive self-concept support—neither of which he may expect to provide or receive. The male Japanese partner may expect to provide self-concept support for his partner's cooking ability, kindness, youth, and honesty as entry variables and to receive self-concept support for his own wealth, fun, honesty, sportsmanship, kindness, and happiness—none of which she may expect to provide or receive (except honesty). Again, honesty would not seem to present a problem at the initiation stage of the relationship, since it is also a crucial attribute for African Americans. As for the European American female and the Japanese male, because the crucial attributes are so dissimilar, initiation of a mate-type relationship between an African American female and a Japanese male would be expected to be quite difficult. Further, if such a relationship is successfully initiated, the results of these studies lead to the speculation that the growth of the relationship may be quite complicated. Although neither partner may expect self-concept support of physical attractiveness to increase, the female African American partner may expect to provide and receive a continuation of self-concept support for sexual appeal and intelligence. She may expect to provide and receive increasing self-concept support of communication, caring, patience, trust, understanding, respect, affection, and support—none of which the Japanese male partner may expect to provide or receive at all. The Japanese male may expect to provide a constant level of self-concept support for his partner's cooking ability, kindness, and youth—none of which she may expect or need—and to receive a constant level of self-concept support for his own wealth, fun, sportsmanship, kindness, and happiness—none of which she may expect to provide. To even further complicate matters, the female African American partner may expect love to continually increase; whereas her Japanese male partner may expect love to increase only at the point when the field is cleared. Finally, the Japanese male partner may expect only to both provide and receive self-concept support for honesty at a constant level; whereas his female African American partner may expect to provide and receive increasing self-concept support for honesty.

These studies suggest that male African American and female Japanese expectations also have almost no similarities. However, like the pairing of European American men with Japanese women, because their dissimilarities are so complete they may be better able to develop sensitivity to them. For both of these samples, physical attractiveness is an entry variable. He may expect to both provide and receive self-concept support on this variable; she only to receive it. For the male African American sample, sexual appeal and intelligence are also entry variables on which they expect to both provide and receive self-concept support—neither of which the Japanese females expect to provide or receive. In addition, the female Japanese partner may expect to provide self-concept support for her partner's wealth, fun, honesty, sportsmanship, kindness, and happiness and to receive self-concept support for her own cooking ability, kindness, youth, and honesty—none of which he may expect to provide or receive (except honesty). Again, honesty does not seem to present a problem at the initiation stage of the relationship, since it is also a crucial attribute for African Americans.

If such a relationship is successfully initiated, the growth of the relationship could be expected to be quite complicated. Although neither partner may expect his self-concept support of her physical attractiveness to increase, the male African American partner may expect to receive a continuation of self-concept support for physical attractiveness (which she may not expect to provide), and he may expect to both provide and receive a continuation of self-concept support for sexual appeal and intelligence—neither of which she may expect to provide or receive. He may expect to provide and receive increasing self-concept support of communication, caring, patience, trust, understanding, respect, affection, and support—none of which the Japanese female partner may expect to provide or receive at all. The Japanese female may expect to provide a constant level of self-concept support for her partner's wealth, fun, sportsmanship, kindness, and happiness and to receive a constant level of self-concept support for her own cooking ability, kindness, and youth—none of which he may expect to receive or to provide, respectively. To even further complicate matters, the male African American partner may expect love to continually increase; whereas his Japanese female partner may expect love to increase only at the point when the field is cleared. The Japanese female partner may expect only to both provide and receive self-concept support for honesty at a constant level; whereas her male African American partner may expect to provide and receive increasing self-concept support for honesty. Finally, the Japanese female may expect to increase her self-concept support for his employment at the point when a public declaration of engagement is made.

Deaf European Americans/non-American mateship pairs. Again, because of the invalidity of the Deaf Culture Galileo data, speculations on the nature of the attributes as entry or intensity variables is not provided. In these data, hearing Jamaican and Deaf European American expectations for mate relationships are similar. Both partners in such a relationship may expect to provide and receive self-concept support for trust, love, honesty, respect, communication, friendship, affection, support, and sexual appeal. The hearing Jamaican partner may also expect to provide and receive self-concept support for understanding, caring, sharing, physical attractiveness, and intelligence; whereas the Deaf partner may expect to provide and receive self-concept support for fun.

Like other American/Japanese pairs, Deaf European American/Japanese pairs have almost no similarities, according to these data. A Deaf European American male may expect to provide and receive self-concept support for fun, honesty, and love. His hearing Japanese female partner may expect to provide and receive self-concept support for honesty and love, but may expect only to provide self-concept support for fun. He may expect to provide and receive self-concept support for communication, affection, support, sexual appeal, trust, friendship, and respect—none of which she may expect to provide or receive. Conversely, she may expect to provide self-concept support for his wealth, sportsmanship, kindness, happiness, and employment—none of which he may expect to receive. She may expect to receive self-concept support for her physical attractiveness, cooking ability, kindness, and youth—none of which he may expect to provide.

A Deaf European American female may expect to provide and receive self-concept support for fun, honesty, and love. Her hearing Japanese male partner may expect to provide and receive self-concept support for honesty and love, but may expect only to receive self-concept support for fun. She may expect to provide and receive self-concept support for communication, affection, support, sexual appeal, trust, friendship, and respect—none of which he may expect to provide or receive. Conversely, he may expect to receive self-concept support for his wealth, sportsmanship, kindness, happiness, and employment—none of which she may expect to provide. He may expect to provide self-concept support for her physical attractiveness, cooking ability, kindness, and youth—none of which she may expect to receive.

Jamaican/Japanese mateship pairs. Jamaican and Japanese expectations for mate relationships are also quite different, according to these studies. Again, because Japanese males and females have such different expectations for providing and receiving self-concept support, we will first consider the pairing of a Jamaican female with a Japanese male. For both of these samples, physical attractiveness is an entry variable. She may expect to both provide and receive self-concept support on this variable; he may only expect to provide it. For the female Jamaican sample, intelligence is also an entry variable on which they expect to both provide and receive self-concept support—neither of which the male Japanese respondents expect to provide or receive. The male Japanese partner may expect to provide self-concept support for his partner's cooking ability, kindness, youth, and honesty as entry variables and expects to receive self-concept support for his own wealth, fun, honesty, sportsmanship, kindness, and happiness—none of which she may expect to provide or receive (except honesty). Honesty does not seem to present a problem at the initiation stage of the relationship, since it is also a crucial attribute for the Jamaican sample. As for other pairings between a Western female and a Japanese male, because the crucial attributes are so dissimilar, initiation of a mate-type relationship may be quite difficult.

Even if such a relationship is successfully initiated, the growth of the relationship may be quite complicated. Although neither partner may expect self-concept support of physical attractiveness to increase, the female Jamaican partner may expect to provide and receive a continuation of self-concept support for intelligence. She may expect to provide and receive increasing self-concept support of trust, respect, communication, understanding, caring, friendship, affection, sharing, support, and sexual appeal—none of which the Japanese male partner may expect to provide or receive at all. The Japanese male may expect to provide a constant level of self-concept support for his partner's cooking ability, kindness, and youth—none of which she may expect or need—and to receive a constant level of self-concept support for his own wealth, fun, sportsmanship, kindness, and happiness—none of which she may expect to provide. To even further complicate matters, the female Jamaican partner may expect love to continually increase; whereas her Japanese male partner may expect love to increase only at the point when the field is cleared. Finally, the Japanese male partner may expect only to both provide and receive self-concept support for honesty at a constant level; whereas his female Jamaican partner may expect to provide and receive increasing self-concept support for honesty.

In these data, male Jamaican and female Japanese expectations also have almost no similarities. However, like the pairing of European American or African American men with Japanese women, because their dissimilarities are so complete they may be better able to develop sensitivity to them. For both of these samples, physical attractiveness is an entry variable. He may expect to both provide and receive self-concept support on this variable; she may only expect to receive it. For the male Jamaican sample, intelligence is also an entry variable on which they expect to both provide and receive self-concept support—neither of which the Japanese females expect to provide or receive. In addition, the female Japanese partner may expect to provide self-concept support for her partner's wealth, fun, honesty, sportsmanship, kindness, and happiness and to receive self-concept support for her own cooking ability, kindness, youth, and honesty—none of which he may expect to provide or receive (except honesty). Again, honesty does not seem to present a problem at the initiation stage of the relationship, since it is a crucial attribute for both samples.

If such a relationship is successfully initiated, the growth of the relationship may be complicated. Although neither partner may expect his self-concept support of her physical attractiveness to increase, the male Jamaican partner may expect to receive a continuation of self-concept support for physical attractiveness (which she may not expect to provide), and he may expect to both provide and receive a continuation of self-concept support for intelligence—which she may expect neither to provide nor receive. He may expect to provide and receive increasing self-concept support of trust, respect, communication, understanding, caring, friendship, affection, sharing, support, and sexual appeal—none of which the Japanese female partner may expect to provide or receive at all. The Japanese female may expect to provide a constant level of self-concept support for her partner's wealth, fun, sportsmanship, kindness, and happiness and to receive a constant level of self-concept support for her own cooking ability, kindness, and youth—none of which he may expect to receive or to provide, respectively. To even further complicate matters, the male Jamaican partner may expect love to continually increase; whereas his Japanese female partner may expect love to increase only at the point when the field is cleared. The Japanese female partner may expect only to both provide and receive self-concept support for honesty at a constant level; whereas her male Jamaican partner may expect to provide and receive increasing self-concept support for honesty. Finally, the Japanese female may expect to increase her self-concept support for his employment at the point when a public declaration of engagement is made.

Looking to the Future

The studies herein are applications of the first four propositions (see Table 1.1) in cultures never before studied in this research tradition. In studies of the United States, the advance made herein is to explicitly overcome the faulty assumption that there is one unified U.S. culture. Three distinct co-cultural groups are examined. The results suggest that these co-cultures are highly similar, but also that they differ in important ways. Numerous U.S. co-cultures—ethnic, regional, economic, and social—have yet to be examined in this way. In addition to enriching our understanding of the United States as a multi-cultural society, two studies herein explored non-U.S. cultures. Interpersonal communication researchers had not previously ventured into the Caribbean region to examine personal relationships. Finally, this theoretic structure had not previously been applied in this way in Japanese culture.

The methodology for identifying and testing crucial attributes that was developed for this research tradition (see Nicotera and Associates 1993) has been firmly upheld as a valuable tool for exploring personal relationship initiation and development cross-culturally. Still, this tradition could be enriched with more interpretive, ethnographic, and longitudinal studies which explore the intricacies of the communication of self-concept support. Further, this body of theory has never been applied to intercultural relationships. Interpretive research would be extremely beneficial in doing so; a substantial enough database of several cultures now exists upon which to base preliminary investigations of intercultural relationships with members from those cultures.

Another contribution of this volume has been to begin exploring with paired-comparison analysis Propositions 5 and 7 (that conflict that threatens self-concept support on crucial relationship variables—the lack of it or attacks on it—is potentially the most dangerous type of conflict in interpersonal relationships; and that quality interpersonal relationships consist of intimacy, personal growth, and effective communication on the crucial relationship variables). These two propositions need to be explored more fully with other types of methodologies. Further, when Proposition 5 is secured, research will be needed to explore Proposition 6 (that negotiation of differences in perceptions of self-concept support on crucial relationship variables cements interpersonal relationships). The results of the present exploratory studies are encouraging. Thus far, Propositions 5 and 7 can be upheld.

The fundamental theory, as summarized in the propositions, could also be enriched for particular cultures with in-depth culturally-specific theory. The histories, values, and belief systems of particular cultures could be theoretically linked with the specific manifestations of the general process identified as cross-culturally applicable in this research tradition. These in-depth cultural analyses could then enrich considerations of intercultural relationships. This theoretic foundation for exploring personal relationship processes offers the potential for encompassing a comprehensive cluster of relational processes—unlike theories limited to particular processes occurring within a faulty assumption of a unified U.S. culture. Finally, as advocated in the final chapter of Nicotera and Associates (1993), the general theory could be deepened paradigmatically by embedding it in a structurational perspective, examining the ways in which cultural rules and resources for the mate relationship are produced and reproduced in interaction. (See Giddens 1984, Bryant and Jary 1991, and Poole, Seibold, and McPhee 1996.)

Yet also to be accomplished is a thorough analysis of how this research tradition fits in with and contributes to the diverse and abundant body of literature on personal relationships. This volume is intended to concentrate on application of the theory to a variety of cultural settings. The work herein is relevant to the literature on relational initiation and growth, conflict at all stages of relationship, relational maintenance and dissolution, and relational quality. Many questions can be raised from the speculations offered in this chapter; heuristic value of these studies is enormous even without attention to the broader literature. With such attention, it is even greater. Because the literature is so broad and diverse and the studies herein so specific and concentrated, it was considered beyond the scope of this volume to do an analysis of the literature. By concentrating on the theory and its application, this volume errs on the side of being too focused on one research tradition. As the purpose was to concentrate on cross-cultural applications of this specific theory, this focus was considered appropriate for this volume. One of the next steps in this research program must be to integrate the knowledge generated by this theory and its application with the broader knowledge in the various areas of research on personal relationships.

REFERENCES

Chapter One

Aguirre, B., & Kirwan, P. (1986). Marriage order and the quality and stability of marital relationships: A test of Lewis and Spanier's theory. *Journal of Comparative Family Studies* *17*, 247–276.

Bailey, R. C., Finney P., and Bailey, K. G. (1974). Level of self-acceptance and perceived intelligence in self and friend. *Journal of Genetic Psychology 124*, 61–67.

Bailey, R. C., Finney, P., and Helm, B. (1975). Self-concept support and friendship. *Journal of Social Psychology 96*, 237–243.

Bailey, R., and Helm, R. (1974). Matrimonial commitment and date/ideal date perception. *Perceptual and Motor Skills 39*, 1356–1357.

Bailey, R. C., and Kelly, M. (1984). Perceived physical attractiveness in early, steady, and engaged daters. *Journal of Psychology 116*, 39-43.

Berger, C. R., and Calabrese, R. (1975). Some explorations in initial interaction and beyond: Toward a developmental theory of interpersonal communication. *Human Communication Research 1*, 99–112.

Berger, C., and Calabrese, R. (1975). Some explorations in initial interaction and beyond: Toward a developmental theory of interpersonal communication. *Human Communication Research 1* 99–112.

Billingham, R. E., and Sack, A. R. (1987). Conflict tactics and the level of emotional commitment among unmarrieds. *Human Relations 40*, 59–74.

Birchler, G.R., Weiss, R.L., and Vincent, J.P. (1975). Multimethod analysis of social reinforcement exchange between maritally distressed and non-distressed spouse and stranger dyads. *Journal of Personality and Social Psychology 31*: 349-60.

Buss, D. M. and Barnes, M. (1986). Preferences in human mate selection. *Journal of Personality and Social Psychology 50*, 559–570.

Cahn, D. D. (1986). *Male-female communication and relationship development: Communication characteristics of mateship stages.* Unpublished paper, State University of New York at New Paltz.

Crawford, M. (1977). What is a Friend? *New Society 42*, 116–117.

Cushman, D. P. (1979). Communication in establishing, maintaining, and terminating interpersonal relationships. *Journal of Youth and Adolescence 8*, 443–452.

Cushman, D. P. (1989). Communication in establishing, maintaining, and terminating interpersonal relationships: A study of mateship. In S. S. King (Ed.), *Human communication as a field of study: Selected contemporary views* (pp. 87– 104). Albany: SUNY Press.

Cushman, D. P., and Cahn, D. D. (1985). *Communication in interpersonal relationships.* Albany: SUNY Press.

Cushman, D. P. and Craig, R. T. (1976). Communication systems: Interpersonal implications. In G. Miller (Ed.), *Explorations in interpersonal communication* (pp. 37–58). Beverly Hills: Sage.

Cushman, D. P., and Florence, B. T. (1974). The development of interpersonal communication theory. *Today's Speech 22*, 11–15.

Cushman, D. P., and Pearce, W. B. (1977). Generality and necessity in three types of communication theory, with special attention to rules theory. *Human Communication Research, 3*, 341–353.

Cushman, D. P., Valentinsen, B., and Dietrich, D. (1982). A rules theory of interpersonal relationships. In F. E. X. Dance (Ed.), *Human Communication Theory* (pp. 90–119). New York: Harper and Row.

Cushman, D. P., and Whiting, G. (1972). An approach to communication theory: Towards consensus on rules. *Journal of Communication 22*, 217–218.

Duck, S. (1976). Interpersonal communication in developing relationships. In G. Miller (Ed.), *Explorations in interpersonal communication* (pp. 127–145). Beverly Hills: Sage.

Fincham, F., and Bradbury, T. (1989). Perceived responsibility for marital events: Egocentric or partner-centric bias? *Journal of Marriage and the Family 51*, 27–35.

Genshaft, J. L. (1980). Perceptual and defensive style variables in marital discord. *Social Behavior and Personality 8*, 81–84.

Gottman, J., Markman, H., and Notarius, C. (1977). The topography of marital conflict: A sequential analysis of verbal and nonverbal behavior. *Journal of Marriage and the Family 39*, 461–447.

Helm, B., Bailey, R., and Vance, B. K. (1977). Interpersonal commitment and self-concept support. *Journal of Social Psychology 102*, 319–320.

Karp, E. S., Jackson, J., and Lester, D. (1970). Ideal-self fulfillment in mate selection: A corollary to the complementary need theory of mate selection. *Journal of Marriage and the Family 32*, 269–272.

Kerckhoff, A. C., and Davis, K. E. (1962). Value consensus and need complementarity in mate selection. *American Sociological Review 27*, 295–303.

Knapp, M. (1978). *Social intercourse: From greeting to goodbye.* Boston: Allyn & Bacon.

Levinger, G. (1980). Toward the analysis of close relationships. *Journal of Experimental Social Psychology 16*, 510–544.

Lewis, R. A. A. (1972). A developmental framework for the analysis of premarital dyadic formation. *Family Process 11*, 17–48.

Lewis, R. A. A. (1973). A longitudinal test of a developmental framework for the analysis of premarital dyadic formation. *Journal of Marriage and the Family 35*, 16–25.

Montgomery, B. M. (1981). The form and function of quality communication in marriage. *Family Relations 30*, 21–29.

Murstein, B. I. (1977). The stimulus-value-role (SVR) theory of dyadic relationships. In S. W. Duck (Ed.), *Theory and Practice in Interpersonal Attraction* (pp. 105–127). London: Academic Press.

Murstein, B. I. (1972). Person perception and courtship progress among premarital couples. *Journal of Marriage and the Family 34*, 621–27.

Nicotera, A.M., and Associates. (1993). *Interpersonal communication in friend and mate relationships*. Albany: SUNY Press.

Nofz, M. P. (1984). Fantasy—testing—assessment: A proposed model for the investigation of mate selection. *Journal of Personality and Social Psychology 50*, 428–438.

Noller, P. (1981). Gender and marital adjustment level differences in decoding messages from spouses and strangers. *Journal of Personality and Social Psychology 41*, 272–278.

Rands, M., Levinger, G., and Mellinger, G. D. (1981). Patterns of conflict resolution and marital satisfaction. *Journal of Family Issues 2*, 297–321.

Rettig, K., and Bubolz, M. (1983). Interpersonal resource exchanges as indicators of quality marriages. *Journal of Marriage and the Family 45*, 497–509.

Ritter, K. Y. (1985). The cognitive therapies. *Journal of Counseling and Development 64*, 42–44.

Spanier, G. B., and Lewis, R. A. (1980). Marital quality: A review of the seventies. *Marriage and Family Living 42*, 825–839.

Ting-Toomey, S. (1983). An analysis of verbal communication patterns in high and low marital adjustment groups. *Human Communication Research 9*, 306–319.

Birchler, G. R., Weiss, R. L., and Vincent, J. P. (1975). Multimethod analysis of social reinforcement exchange between maritally distressed and nondistressed spouse and stranger dyads. *Journal of Personality and Social Psychology 31*, 349–360.

Chapter Two

Asante, M. K., and Davis, A. (1989). Encounters in the interracial workplace. In M. K. Asante and W. B. Gudykunst (Eds.), *Handbook of international and intercultural communication* (pp. 374–391). Newbury Park, CA: Sage.

Collier, M. J. (1988). A comparison of conversations among and between domestic culture groups: How intra- and intercultural competiencies vary. *Communication Quarterly 36*, 122–144.

Collier, M. J. (1991). Conflict competence within African, Mexican, and Anglo American friendships. In S. Ting-Toomey and F. Korzenny (Eds.), *International and Intercultural Communication Annual* (Vol. 15, pp. 32–54). Newbury Park, Cal.: Sage.

Cushman, D. P., and Cahn, D. D. (1985). *Communication in interpersonal relationships*. Albany: SUNY Press.

Hecht, M. L., Collier, M.J., and Ribeau, S. (1993). *African American communication: Ethnic identity and cultural interpretations*. Newbury Park, Cal.: Sage.

Hecht, M. L., Larkey, L.K., and Johnson, J.N. (1992). African American and European American perceptions of problematic issues in interethnic communiation effectiveness. *Human Communication Research 19*, 209–236.

Hecht, M. L., and Ribeau, S. (1984). Ethnic communication: A comparative analysis of satisfying communication. *International Journal of Intercultral Relations 8*, 135–151.

Hecht, M. L., and Ribeau, S. (1987). Afro-American identity labels and communicative effectiveness. *Journal of Language and Social Psychology 6*, 319–326.

Hecht, M. L., Ribeau S., and Alberts, J. K. (1989). An Afro-American perspective on interethnic communication. *Communication Monographs 56*, 385–410.

Hecht, M. L., Ribeau, S., and Sedano, M. V. (1990). A Mexican-American perspective on interethnic communication. *International Journal of Intercultral Relations 14*, 31–55.

Keane-Dawes, J. (1995). *A critical interpretive approach to stigma: Variation in responses of culturally diverse Jamaican and American deaf groups*. Unpublished doctoral dissertation. Howard University, Washington, D.C.

Martin, J. N., Hecht, M. L., and Larkey, L.K. (1994). Conversational improvement strategies for interethnic communication: African American and European American perspectives. *Communication Monographs 61*, 236–255.

Nicotera, A. M., and Associates. (1993). *Interpersonal communication in friend and mate relationships*. Albany: SUNY Press.

Shuter, R. (1982). Initial interaction of American blacks and whites in interracial and intraracial dyads. *The Journal of Socual Psychology 117*, 45–52.

Chapter Three

Cushman, D. P., and Cahn, D. D. (1985). *Communication in interpersonal relationships.* Albany: SUNY Press.

Gudykunst, W. B., and Hammer, M. R. (1987). The influence of ethnicity, gender, and dyadic composition on uncertainty reduction in initial interaction. *Journal of Black Studies 18*, 191–214.

Hecht, M. L., Collier, M. J., and Ribeau, S. (1993). *African American communication: Ethnic identity and cultural interpretations.* Newbury Park, Cal.: Sage.

Hecht, M. L., and Ribeau, S. (1984). Ethnic communication: A comparative analysis of satisfying communication. *International Journal of Intercultral Relations 8,* 135–151.

Hofstede, G. (1980). *Culture's consequences: International differences in work-related values.* Beverly Hills: Sage.

Jenkins, A. H. (1982). *The psychology of the Afro-American: A humanistic approach.* New York: Pergamon.

Kochman, T. (1982). *Black and white styles in conflict.* Chicago: University of Chicago Press.

LaFrance, M., and Mayo, C. (1976). Racial differences in gaze behavior during conversations: Two systematic observational studies. *Journal of Personality and Scoial Psychology 33*, 547–552.

Martin, J. N., Hecht, M .L., and Larkey, L. K. (1994). Conversational improvement strategies for interethnic communication: African American and European American perspectives. *Communication Monographs 61*, 236–255.

Nicotera, A. M. and Associates. (1993). *Interpersonal communication in friend and mate relationships.* Albany: SUNY Press.

Rose, L. F. R. (1982/3). Theoretical and methodological issues in the study of Black culture and personality. *Humboldt Journal of Social Relations 13*, 320–338.

White, J. L., and Parham, T. A. (1990). *The psychology of Blacks: An African-American perspective.* Englewood Cliffs, N.J.: Prentice Hall.

Chapter Four

Cohen, H. L. (1994). *Train go sorry: Inside a deaf world.* Boston: Houghton Mifflin.

Cushman, D. P., and Cahn, D. D. (1985). *Communication in interpersonal relationships.* Albany: SUNY Press.

Dolnick, E. (1993, September). Deafness as a culture. *The Atlantic Monthly,* pp. 37–53.

Higgins, P. (1980). *Outsiders in a hearing world: A sociology of deafness.* Beverly Hills: Sage.

Keane-Dawes, J. (1995). *A critical interpretive approach to stigma: Variation in responses of culturally diverse Jamaican and American deaf groups.* Unpublished doctoral dissertation. Howard University, Washington, D.C.

Nicotera, A. M., and Associates. (1993). *Interpersonal communication in friend and mate relationships.* Albany: SUNY Press.

Norman, J. (1995). *"(Un)Reasonable Doubts": Selective exposure and selective perception.* Unpublished doctoral dissertation. Howard University, Washington, D.C.

Padden, C., and Humphries, T. (1988). *Deaf in America: Voices from a culture.* Cambridge: Harvard University Press.

Chapter Five

Keane-Dawes, J. (1995). *A critical interpretive approach to stigma: Variation in responses of culturally diverse Jamaican and American deaf groups.* Unpublished doctoral dissertation. Howard University, Washington, D.C.

Manley, M. (1990). *The politics of change: A Jamaican treatment.* Washington, D.C.: Howard University Press.

Chapter Six

Cushman, D. P., and Cahn, D. D. (1985). *Communication in interpersonal relationships*. Albany: SUNY Press.

Cushman, D. P., Valentinsen, B., and Dietrich, D. (1982). A rules theory of interpersonal relationships. In F. E. X. Dance (Ed.), *Human Communication Theory* (pp. 90–119). New York: Harper and Row.

Nicotera, A. M. and Associates. (1993). *Interpersonal communication in friend and mate relationships*. Albany: SUNY Press.

Chapter Seven

Kochman, T. (1982). *Black and white styles in conflict*. Chicago: University of Chicago Press.

Martin, J. N., Hecht, M. L., and Larkey, L. K. (1994). Conversational improvement strategies for interethnic communication: African American and European American perspectives. *Communication Monographs 61*, 236–255.

Nicotera, A. M., and Associates. (1993). *Interpersonal communication in friend and mate relationships*. Albany: SUNY Press.

Chapter Eight

Nicotera, A. M., and Associates. (1993). *Interpersonal communication in friend and mate relationships*. Albany: SUNY Press.

Chapter Nine

Bryant, C. G. A. and Jary, D. (1991). *Giddens' theory of structuration: A critical appreciation*. New York: Routledge.

Chu, G. C. (1979). Communication and cultural change in China: A conceptual framework. In G. C. Chu and F. L. K. Hsu (Eds.), *Moving a mountain: cultural change in China* (pp. 2–24). Honolulu: The University Press of Hawaii.

Chu, G. C. (1985). The changing concept of self in contemporary China. In A. J. Marsella, G. DeVos, and F. L. K. Hsu (Eds.), *Culture and Self: Asian and Western Perspectives* (pp. 252–277). New York: Tavistock Publications.

Davis, L. E., and Strube, M. J. (1993). An assessment of romantic commitment among Black and White dating couples. *Journal of Applied Social Psychology 23*, 212–225.

Giddens, A. (1984). *The constitution of society: Outline of a theory of structuration.* Berkeley: University of California Press.

Kochman, T. (1982). *Black and white styles in conflict.* Chicago: University of Chicago Press.

Lewis, R., Robinson, C., and Yancy, G. (1995). *Mate selection among interracial couples.* Paper presented at the annual meeting of the Society for the Study of Social Problems.

Martin, J. N., Hecht, M. L., and Larkey, L. K. (1994). Conversational improvement strategies for interethnic communication: African American and European American perspectives. *Communication Monographs 61*, 236–255.

Nicotera, A. M., and Associates. (1993). *Interpersonal communication in friend and mate relationships.* Albany: SUNY Press.

Poole, M. S., Seibold, D. R., and McPhee, R. (1996). The structuration of group decisions. In R. Y. Hirokawa and M. S. Poole (Eds.), *Communication and group decision making.* (pp. 114–146). Thousand Oaks, CA:Sage.

INDEX